21 ARMY GROUP ORDNANCE

THE STORY OF THE CAMPAIGN
IN NORTH WEST EUROPE

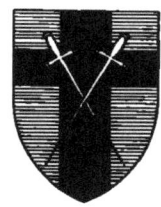

21 ARMY GROUP ORDNANCE

THE STORY OF THE CAMPAIGN IN NORTH WEST EUROPE

The Naval & Military Press Ltd

By
MAJOR J. LEE-RICHARDSON, R.A.O.C.

(Illustrations by Sgt. W. Savage, R.A.O.C.)

Published by

The Naval & Military Press Ltd
Unit 5 Riverside, Brambleside
Bellbrook Industrial Estate
Uckfield, East Sussex
TN22 1QQ England

Tel: +44 (0)1825 749494

www.naval-military-press.com
www.nmarchive.com

*In reprinting in facsimile from the original, any imperfections are inevitably reproduced
and the quality may fall short of modern type and cartographic standards.*

FOREWORD

by the
DIRECTOR OF ORDNANCE SERVICES
21 ARMY GROUP

THIS RECORD was designed as a popular and readable History of the work of the Ordnance Services of 21 Army Group.

It is impossible to do full justice to the large number of Ordnance units, of varying importance and size, which made their contribution to the ultimate success of the Ordnance Services as a whole.

At the same time, this story does place on record some of the outstanding feats performed, and lessons learned, in a truly remarkable campaign.

I feel it will be treasured by all who took part, both as a souvenir of strenuous but thrilling days and as a reminder of the "esprit de corps" which animated all ranks and led them on to play an important part in the ultimate design of Victory.

Major-General, D.O.S.

Views of 15 Advanced Base Ordnance Depot, Antwerp

CONTENTS

CHAPTER   PAGE

I. The Invasion is Planned

Early general discussions and conferences which prepared for the projected "Second Front". Planning begins to take more concrete form. Appointment of Brigadier Denniston as D.O.S. 21 Army Group. The intensive efforts made in the Central Ordnance Depots. Changes in the Ordnance Organisation for supply in the field. Regimental training, embracing beach landings, etc. Y-day draws near   9

II. Getting Ready for D-day

Role of Ordnance with the Assault Corps. Introduction of landing reserves and beach maintenance packs. Training of the four Advanced Ordnance Depots and Base Ammunition Depots. Preparation of Ordnance Beach Detachments, Ordnance Ammunition Companies, etc. The Second Army Ordnance "Appreciation of the Situation". How the Appreciation was fulfilled.   14

III. The Dawn of D-day

Situation at 21 Army Group on D—1. The first "Situation Reports" confirm our highest hopes. Successful landings by the O.B.D.'s and O.A.C.'s. Formation of the Beach Sub Areas and the part Ordnance played in them. D-day adventures of Ordnance Units. Landing of the first ammunition supplies and setting up of dumps behind the beaches   19

IV. The Campaign Unfolds : Normandy to Antwerp

Ordnance Beach Units move inshore. Advanced elements of succeeding Ordnance Units begin to arrive. Withdrawal of the O.B.D.'s and setting up of the first A.O.D. and B.A.D. Early efforts to recover returned stores by the Ordnance Maintenance Company. Laundries and Bath Units begin to arrive. Problems of the great break-through. Formation of Ordnance Stores Convoy Unit. 21 Army Group "Appreciation of the Situation". How the plan worked. List of first Ordnance Field Parks in the theatre. Lengthening of the L of C and its problems. Setting up of new depots as L of C develops. Serving the Army in highly mobile warfare   26

V. The Story of the Advanced Ordnance Depots

Planning and preparation of the A.O.D.'s. Disaster overtakes the first A.O.D. Recce Party. Reserve Recce Party arrives and confirms sites chosen in first "key" plan. How the first Advanced Depot was organised. Armies maintained by this Depot till D + 100. Formation of second Advanced Ordnance Depot. A difficult site presents many problems, successfully overcome. Maintenance of the Army by this Depot during the sweep to Belgium. Formation of the third A.O.D. at Antwerp. Details of the immense tonnages and wide range of stores. Clearing the Rear Maintenance Area. Formation of Advanced B.O.D. Setting up the "Run-down" Depot. The story of the Vehicle Parks   34

CHAPTER		PAGE
VI.	**Keeping the Army on Wheels**	
	Formation of the Vehicle Companies. Planning in England prior to D-day. How the first vehicles were landed. The Vehicle Park organisation in the bridgehead. Parks formed in echelon along the L of C. Vehicle Companies split from the Advanced Ordnance Depot. The range of vehicles stocked. Waterproofing and de-waterproofing. Vehicle Parks opened in the Advanced Base. Some interesting facts and stories behind the Vehicle supply organisation.	39
VII.	**Pass the Ammunition !**	
	Small beach ammunition dumps are superseded by the first Base Ammunition Depot. Arrival of the B.A.D. Advance Parties. Sniping, shelling and bombing of the ammunition sites. Transport of ammunition over the beaches by Dukws. Sites selected for 17 B.A.D. and 15 B.A.D. Shelling of beaches enforces a temporary abandonment of discharging. Enemy drops sea-mines in ammunition depots. Crisis caused by a bad turn in the weather. Several thousand mines explode "en masse". Tremendous tonnages handled. Ammunition Depots set up in echelon as L of C expands. Heavy congestion in the beachhead. Formation of Ammunition Roadheads and their part in various operations.	43
VIII.	**On to the Rhine and the Baltic**	
	Recapitulation of the situation after the fall of Antwerp. The original plans and build-up for the invasion of Germany. Problems raised by the Ardennes counter-offensive. Ordnance planning for the clearance of the Reichswald Forest (Operation—"Veritable"). Special Stores for the Rhine crossing (Operation—"Plunder"). The part played by Ordnance Field Parks in both these operations. The pursuit to the Baltic. Capitulation of the enemy and the new problems which arose.	49
IX.	**Specialist Ordnance Units**	
	Details of the work done by the Base and Base Hospital Laundries, Bath Units, Industrial Gas Units, Armoured Stores Company, Forward Maintenance Stores and Ammunition Sections, Ordnance Maintenance Companies, Forward Trailer Sections, Ammunition Repair Units, D.A.D.O.S. Dumps, RAOC Convoy Units, Officers' Shops, Provision by Local Resources, Depot Control Companies etc. A record of achievements.	57
X.	**Ordnance for the Airborne Landings**	
	Planning the Ordnance side of the Airborne Operations for 21 Army Group. The Plot for D-eve landings. Ordnance representatives drop with supplies. How "airborne" stores are scaled and dropped. Holding the vital Orne bridgehead. Preparations for the Arnhem drop. Ordnance Representatives suffer heavy casualties. The airborne operation for the Rhine crossing.	66
XI.	**Canada's Stirring Contribution**	
	The part played by the Royal Canadian Ordnance Corps. Planning for D-day. The first Canadian Ordnance units arrive. Exploiting the Falaise Gap. The transport problems and how they were met. Ordnance preparations for clearing the Scheldt, Walcheren and South Beveland. Clearing the approach to the Rhine. Canadian Ordnance Units which took part throughout the campaign.	73
XII.	**R.A.O.C. Honours and Awards**	
	Honours and awards made to Ordnance personnel in 21 Army Group. R.A.O.C. Group of Battle.	78

LIST OF ILLUSTRATIONS

	PAGE
Views of 15 Advanced Base Ordnance Depot	4
Chart of the Invasion Beaches	18
LST Sails on D-day	23
Beach Maintenance Packs at 17 AOD .	27
17 AOD Gun Park near Vaux-sur-Aure	31
Wintry Conditions at 14 AOD.	35
A Park of 17 Vehicle Company, near Vaux-sur-Aure	41
12 BAD in Normandy	45
The first Base Laundry at Vaucelles	45
Stores Section at No. 6 Army Roadhead at Enghien	48
A heavy "A" Vehicle Park	48
Glimpses of an Ordnance Field Park	55
Forward Trailer Section near Bayeux	55
A Mobile Laundry Unit at Work	59
No. 1 Base Industrial Gas Unit	59
Map of Locations of RAOC Units	95

21 ARMY GROUP ORDNANCE

CHAPTER I

THE INVASION IS PLANNED

"GENERAL MONTGOMERY now stands at the head of a very large and powerful army, *equipped as no Army has ever been equipped before.* When I last saw him in the field he used these words which he authorised me to repeat if I chose. He said 'I doubt if the British War Office has ever sent an Army overseas so well equipped as the one now fighting in Normandy'."

The speaker is Mr. Winston Churchill. The place is the House of Commons. The occasion is one of the great historic reviews of the war, which he was in the habit of making at intervals. The date is Tuesday, August 3rd 1944.

And where are our Armies ? While Mr. Churchill is speaking, they are smashing the whole German front running south-west of Villers Bocage. The great break-through has come, eclipsing in its power and breadth our very wildest hopes. With characteristic insight, in foreshadowing this staggering blow, the Prime Minister has put his finger on the vital subject of supplies.

Supplies—the life blood of an Army ! With the exception only of food, fuel, drugs, stationery and certain engineering stores, Ordnance has the job of ensuring that the needed Stores and Ammunition are there, in sufficient quantity, and at the right time and place, when the Army needs them. The variety of these supplies is bewildering, ranging from a toothbrush to a tank, from a round of ammunition to a radiolocation range-finder.

The waging of a modern war absorbs immense quantities of material, much of it highly technical, all of it wanted urgently. That is why Ordnance services do influence the course of battles in a measure quite impossible to exaggerate. The particular operation which involved a mass landing in France demanded exceptional foresight, training, experience and skill.

Only a few weeks previously, Mr. Churchill had told the House of the fateful invasion : "During the night and early hours of June 6th, the first of a series of landings in force upon the European continent has taken place." Again he stressed the importance of stores and equipment, and said that nothing which could be done had been neglected.

It was a testing time for Ordnance, in common with the other arms and services. Here was the largest undertaking it had ever faced, as well as being by far the most critical. For months the Ordnance Staffs at War Office, 21st Army Group, the Second British Army and the Canadian First Army had been working against the clock to prepare for it. For months our great Central Ordnance Depots at home, employing scores of thousands of workers, had been engaged in amassing the necessary stores.

Our story begins before April 1943, although that was a "key" date in all Invasion planning. That was the date when a British and American Planning Staff was formed, at the decision of the Combined Chiefs of Staff Committee, especially to prepare the actual plan for the invasion of France. This plan, which selected the beaches for the attack, was shown by Mr. Churchill to Mr. Roosevelt at the famous conference at Quebec. Later, it was taken by the Prime Minister to Teheran, where Marshal Stalin was appraised of the details. At Teheran Mr. Churchill told Stalin that the operation would be put into effect "at the end of May or the beginning of June, 1944."

But even before April, 1943, when the first concrete invasion planning was begun, Ordnance obligations in the Second Front were being studied. The Controller of Ordnance Services, Major-General Sir Leslie H. Williams K.B.E., C.B., M.C., had directed that the whole Ordnance "set-up" for supply in the field should be revised. The framework was to be re-modelled for an invasion involving a short sea voyage. Not only the chain of supply, but such matters as the actual packing of the invasion stores, were considered in detail. In all these matters, experience gained in contested landings in the Mediterranean was turned to good account. We had to visualise an operation which would involve the heaviest fighting on a narrow strip of shore devoid of docks and under continuous fire.

Speed would be the ascendant factor—speed in discharging stores at sea, speed in transporting them over the beaches, speed in sorting and stacking: above all, speed on making the needed issues. A special type of box was evolved in which pre-cartoned stores were packed and waterproofed. This box was designed to be used as a bin in the field without the items having to be unpacked. An ingenious but simplified form of accounting and locating was developed.

Appointment of Commanders

In January, 1944, matters took a new turn when the Commanders of the Invasion Force were appointed. Fresh impetus was given to the spade work: a new sense of urgency filled the air. 21 Army Group had grown out of GHQ. Home Forces, and Brigadiers C.A.N. Swiney and H. King had served as the original Directors of Ordnance Services, with Col. J. R. M. Cape as D.D.O.S. Brigadier J. G. Denniston assumed in January, 1944, the appointment of Director of Ordnance Services 21 Army Group, where Col. L. E. Cutforth was already acting as D.D.O.S. Both continued in these capacities throughout the whole of "Operation Overlord," as the invasion preparations became secretly known. They were thus destined to see the fulfilment of the plan on which they expended so much effort and thought during the first six months of 1944.

And what a plan! Five successful opposed landings had taken place previously in the Middle East theatre. The lessons of these were studied at length. Staff tables were prepared, Scales for the maintenance of the Force were revised. Wastage rates for all types of vehicles, major assemblies and technical equipment were collated. Weights and shipping tables were worked out. The Order of Battle was evolved. Roles were assigned to the Ordnance units singled out to accompany the assault spearheads. And while these and a thousand other problems were being studied at Army levels, two other things were happening.

Side by side with this vast administrative detail, the RAOC personnel of 21 Army Group units were being trained in the Field, and the stores for the forthcoming operation were being selected and packed in the Depots.

Battle Training Begins

From the first, the D.O.S. decided that regimental training should have priority in the preparation of Ordnance units for this most crucial of all Invasions. His target was to turn out men who were as physically fit and regimentally ready, as they were technically sound, for their role. Various tactical exercises and schemes were therefore introduced, including landings from assault craft on hotly defended strips of coast, the transport of stores across beachheads under fire, and the handling of receipts and issues in improvised "dumps" amid truly warlike conditions.

Meanwhile, in the Central Ordnance Depots, the preparation of Landing Reserve Sets and Beach Maintenance Packs went forward with an ever increasing tempo. Sir James Grigg, as War Minister, partly lifted the veil on this immense undertaking when he disclosed in the House of Commons some figures indicating the traffic in stores which took place in the two months preceding D-day. During that time, he said, "twelve thousand armoured fighting vehicles, sixty thousand lorries, and two million spare parts were issued by the Ordnance Depots." Nobly they fulfilled their task, working late hours, abandoning all holidays and leave, so that the two thousand odd units which were ultimately to compose 21 Army Group should be fully equipped on time, with reserves of maintenance stores pre-packed to follow through. In fact, leave was for many months suspended throughout the Corps.

From the point of view of the Directorate at Army Group, the invasion planning fell broadly under four headings :—

Primarily, mobilising, training and equipping Ordnance Units in the Army Group.

Secondly, deciding the order in which these units were to be landed, where they would land and at what stage in the operations the landing should take place. Many of the units were so large that they had to be broken down into small component parts, and "phased in" piece-meal. This also applied to their war equipment, which was considerable, and such items as cranes, for example, presented difficult problems as regards transport, loading and shipment.

Thirdly, the maintenance of the force. This problem was complicated by changes in the Order of Battle which took place even during the later stages of the planning.

The scaling of M.T. and technical stores for Ord Field Parks, Workshop Stores Sections, Landing Reserves, Beach Maintenance Packs and auto-maint packs for A.O.D.'s was the responsibility of the REME Scales Branches. Similar work for Clothing and General Stores was the responsibility of the D.C.S. Scales Branch.

In the case of Ord Field Parks and Stores Sections with REME Workshops, from the moment that the initial scaling was received, adjustments in the stock holding were made in the light of experience in consultation with REME, and Signals Officers in formations, and this resulted in greatly increased availability and the elimination of stocks which proved to be slow-moving.

Shipping Shortages

Early in the planning it was found quite impossible to land, in the requisite period, complete LR's for formations which would be ashore, and it therefore fell to D D O S. Second Army to decide which parts of LR's it would be best to ship, having regard to the tonnage available. Similar decisions had to be made by D O S. 21 Army Group in the case of the much heavier BMP's, and it also fell to him to decide upon what additional and special LR's and BMP's were required over and above those prepared for the normal formations, and to arrange with War Office for their preparation.

In addition to BMP's, it was necessary to phase in "bricks" of accommodation stores, stores required by the RAMC, such as stretchers and blankets etc.

In the case of auto-maint packs for the A.O.D., the order in which the various parts were to be shipped had to be decided in the light of the tonnage available, taking into consideration the importance of the stores, the order in which they were likely to be required and the time it would take to stock the depot ready for issue.

There were certain other special classes of stores to be dealt with. Stores for special signal projects known as S.O. in C's Reserves (SOCR) were decided upon by the Signal Officer in Chief, and arrangements for packing, shipping and separate stocking in the A.O.D. were made by D.O.S.

Requirements of Ordnance stores for RE Works Services and Transportation stores, were stated respectively by the Director of Works and Director of Transportation, and after vetting, the list of their requirements was passed by D.O.S. to War Office for packing and shipping direct to Engineer Store Base Depots and Tn Base Depots. Shipping bids for these stores were the responsibility of the user service.

Bidding and Co-ordination

In the early days, bids for shipping space had to be made as far ahead as six weeks in advance of the sailing dates ! Space was at a premium, and the sum-total of the bids usually represented twice as much shipping as the Services had been allocated. Often the original bids had to be halved, which meant re-considering the scaling afresh, deciding what could most safely and conveniently be phased-back to a later date, and generally "streamlining" the original plans.

Finally, all this planning and review had to be co-ordinated so that, for example, stores did not arrive at beaches, or on dates, when the necessary Ordnance organisation for their receipt and issue was not already available to handle them. Much depended on the decisions embodied in the First Key Plan. This was a tracing, showing how the various Ordnance units would be disposed in the projected beachhead. The plan was built up from a study of maps and air photographs, and was subject, of course, to modification as a result of the first recce, of the actual ground.

Although much of the detailed planning fell to the lot of the Ordnance Directorate at 21 Army Group, similar work was taking place at lower formations. Second Army was charged with the original assault, and the Ordnance Staff of Second Army were consequently responsible for the detailed and administrative planning covering this vital phase. Army Group was to regain control after D+17, and whereas Second Army plans covered D-day to D+17 the Army Group plans formed before D-day centred around the period between D+17 and D+70—a task which the most competent of planners might shirk, since so much depended on the unforseeable happenings which would occur in the Beachhead from the time of the assault up to D+17.

Nearing Zero Hour

As D-day approached, however, Ordnance representatives at all levels became ever more busily occupied with the detailed plots for the units assigned to them. What was happening at the Ordnance Directorate at 21 Army Group and at Second. Army, was also taking place at lower levels of command. The D. Ds. O. S. of Corps, the A. Ds. O. S. of Divisions, right down to the Brigade Ordnance Warrant Officers of Brigades, all now played their part in putting together the pieces of the immense jig-saw of planning that had been conceived and designed at Army Group level. The rest of the Army has very little conception of the manifold problems involved in the provision and supply of vast quantities of stores such as were needed for this historic battle. No allowance could be made, nor would any explanation be accepted, if the items required were not available when wanted, and the Ordnance representatives at every level of command simply had to see to it that the Army Group policy and timetable covered and anticipated their every need. After all, the Ordnance service is judged, not by its success in managing vast organisations or in handling staggering tonnages. It is judged by its customers on the service it gives them, irrespective of *how* that service is made. For "Operation Overlord", the service simply had to be as perfect and all-embracing as human ingenuity could contrive.

So this work of planning, scaling, training and equipping went steadily on. Nor was "Operation Overlord" the only scheme which occupied the Ordnance Directorate at Army Group during these fateful days. Another scheme had to be planned—"Operation Rankin"—which was the plan to occupy Germany in the event of that country capitulating. Such is the optimism of the British people that, even at this period when Germany was in absolute command of Europe, provision was already being made to assume control in the event of her sudden surrender. However, this early preparation for a German capitulation was not entirely wasted. It was to prove a valuable exercise for the planning of "Operation Overlord."

Changes of Plan

Meanwhile, as time went on, "Operation Overlord" became more and more the main pre-occupation. Plans were made, shelved, taken out of cold storage, modified, re-cast, quashed and then revised again! This frequent amendment was due mainly to alterations in principle and policy at a high operational level. The size and composition of the Force were constantly under review. Roles assigned to certain formations were in a state of flux. All these second thoughts on policy and principle, implemented by the "G" Staff, necessarily had their impact upon the Ordnance measures to supply the needed stores. At one stage, detailed plans were complete, based on the assumption that one Assault Corps would make the initial invasion. Then it was decided to double the force, so once again the Ordnance plans had to be framed anew. A major problem always was to obtain finality in the Order of Battle.

Occasionally this planning had its lighter side, and sometimes owing to the need of absolute secrecy, the best jokes were appreciated by only a few people "in the know." One such occured at the RAOC Training Establishment, Leicester. The D.O.S. had arranged to call his officers together there for a conference, so that everyone could meet his opposite numbers. Part of the proceedings was a lecture on beach maintenance, and the Training Establishment were asked to get ready a map showing a piece of coastline, for demonstration purposes.

Arriving at Leicester on the night before the conference, a senior Officer of 21 Army Group thought he would like to see this map. He was horrified to discover that the coastline chosen was the exact strip of Normandy where the British landings were planned to take place—indeed, the strip which Mr. Churchill had shown in great secrecy to Mr. Roosevelt and Marshal Stalin only a few months before!

The harrassed officer hurriedly sought the artist, declared the map unsatisfactory and instructed that another be prepared. Duly mortified, the artist retired from the scene, astounted that his efforts had fallen so short of the high aesthetic standards of the Ordnance Directorate!

At this time, the target date for the completion of all the invasion plans was known as Y-day. This was the 31st May, 1944. By that date, everything had to be ready—even to the stage where ships were pre-loaded to sail at a moment's notice, and units concentrated near the coast in readiness to embark.

As the target date approached, a crisis arose in connection with the waterproofing of vehicles and equipments. Until ports were captured on the French coast, vehicles would have to be driven direct from landing craft over the beaches. Certain types of vehicles did not waterproof successfully, and a new method of waterproofing had to be devised at short notice. Due to difficulties in getting the necessary materials, the waterproofing programme was seriously delayed and urgent and drastic measures had to be taken. Thanks, however, to quite exceptional efforts, the required number of vehicles were successfully waterproofed, and a situation which at one stage looked so serious that D-day might have to be postponed, was fortunately averted.

Final Moves

The Rear HQ of Second Army moved a month before Y-day to Fort Purbrook, near Portsmouth; the Canadian First Army and the L of C Units also moved to their sealed concentration compounds. The Ordnance "Appreciation" was published, and as the end of May approached, the RAOC staffs were privileged to see their carefully laid schemes swiftly and surely approaching finality, despite last minute changes of policy.

By 31st May, in fact, everything *was* ready. The future, with all its hazards, looked less menacing as they surveyed the fruits of all this planning and preparation, and awaited in high suspense the fateful word "Go"!

CHAPTER II

GETTING READY FOR D-DAY

TO understand in full the preparations for the June offensive, it is necessary to examine the special roles assigned to the Advanced Ordnance Depots, Base Ammunition Depots, and the various smaller Ordnance units which were to play their part in the initial phase of "Operation Overlord".

The two assault Corps which were chosen to make the first landings were both drawn from the British Second Army. They were 1 and 30 Corps respectively. The D. D's. O. S. of these Corps were accordingly charged with responsibility for all Ordnance units landing up to and including D+1. In addition to their own Corps Troops and Divisional Ordnance units, they had under command several Ordnance Beach Detachments, Ordnance Ammunition Companies, Port Ordnance Detachments and Port Ammunition Detachments.

The assault was to be carried out on a three Divisional front, and it was the intention to form as soon as possible three "Beach Sub Areas". Therefore, the Stores and Ammunition Sections of the Ordnance Beach Detachments in each Beach Sub Area were amalgamated to handle all Ordnance stores and ammunition flowing into their respective beach sub areas. The stores were scaled and packed as "Landing Reserves"—broadly speaking, enough stores of all types to cover the intensive operational needs of an Infantry Brigade for fifteen days. "Beach Maintenance Packs" were to follow the Landing Reserves, and to go direct to the Advanced Ordnance Depot. Again speaking broadly, the "packs" were scaled to the operational requirements of a Division, and obviously included a much larger quantity of stores, as well as a wider range of items.

The plan, therefore, was to supply the theatre with stores through the Ordnance Beach Detachments by means of Landing Reserves in the first phase; and through the Advanced Ordnance Depot by means of Beach Maintenance Packs in the second. Similarly with ammunition, the Ordnance Beach Detachment Ammunition Sections and the Ordnance Ammunition Companies, etc., were to land with the assault troops, while the Base Ammunition Depot would follow later to open up a full scale organisation as the needs of the theatre expanded.

How were the various Ordnance units earmarked? How were they prepared for their task? What units were chosen?

Ordnance Stores Arrangements

Within the establishment of 21 Army Group there were four Advanced Ordnance Depots. These Depots (Nos. 14, 15, 16 and 17 A. O. Ds.) were formed in England specially for 21 Army Group, and underwent intensive and arduous training, both regimental and technical. Early in January, 1944 (D—120) the D. O. S. decided that 17 Advanced Ordnance Depot would be the first to be phased in for operations and that it should operate with beach maintenance packs which could be stacked in the open. The technical training of this Depot, which had previously been concerned with normal A. O. D. procedure, was therefore immediately switched to beach maintenance packs. Personnel attached to Central Ordnance Depots assisted in the preparation of these packs and in due course all companies of the Advanced Ordnance Depot were concentrated at Apley Park, Wellington, the move being completed in April, 1944. About this time the D.O.S. directed that 17 Advanced Ordnance Depot should be assisted by the Stores Companies of 16 Advanced Ordnance Depot in view of the magnitude of their task, and these companies therefore immediately passed under the command of the Chief Ordnance Officer, 17 Advanced Ordnance Depot.

Exercise "Snowball," in which both Advanced Ordnance Depots co-operated, was carried out under Field conditions, with the assistance of Pioneer Companies which had been allocated to 17 Advanced Ordnance Depot. This exercise, when a complete beach maintenance pack was employed, gave all personnel valuable practical experience in receiving, stacking and issuing stores under the conditions they were expected to meet in the forthcoming operation.

It also conclusively proved that Beach Maintenance Packs could not be stacked and issued in the theatre on a Formation basis. The "packs" were scaled to cover the needs of specific Formations, but as a result of the experience gained in this Exercise it was decided to "pool" the packs and ship them across to be stacked and issued not on a Formation but on an equipment and type of vehicle basis. From this common pool, based on the consolidated holdings of all Formations, the whole Force would be supplied.

Meanwhile, the other Advanced Ordnance Depots carried on normal regimental and technical training, and the plan which D.O.S. had agreed was that 14 Advanced Ordnance Depot should be available to "leap-frog" over the initial Advanced Ordnance Depot ; while 15 Advanced Ordnance Depot were to remain in hand for any unforeseen emergency.

On 13 May 1944 (D—23), 17 and 16 Advanced Ordnance Depots moved to their Concentration Areas, where their regimental training continued until the move to the Marshalling Area was made on D—8. By this time the men in all the Advanced Ordnance Depots had reached an exceptionally high peak of physical fitness, and had complete confidence in their ability to carry out the technical tasks to which they were allotted.

Ammunition Arrangements

Several Base Ammunition Depots were called into being, but once again it was No. 17 which drew lucky ! In common with others, this Depot had been mobilised specially for the landing in France. Its personnel were given intensive battle drill. They were attached to Beach Groups for training in connection with beach landings, which included assault landings and the laying-out of beach ammunition dumps.

With other Ordnance units, this Depot acquired much useful experience by participating in Exercise "Jantzen". The exercise took place under realistic conditions in Wales and provided training in the clearance of ammunition ferried over the beaches, and the maintenance of issues after the initial landing.

From February, 1944 onwards, all Ammunition Companies belonging to 17 Base Ammunition Depot were permanently attached to the Beach Groups for training, and their concentration and embarkation were carried out with these Groups. Meanwhile, the other Base Ammunition Depots were undergoing similar rigorous training in anticipation of playing an important role in the future combined operations.

The Small Units

Mention has been made of the smaller Ordnance units which were earmarked for work in maintaining the spearheard forces. These units functioned in the original, vital hours and days. They were the Ordnance Beach Detachments, Port Ordnance and Ammunition Detachments, and detachments of the Divisional Ordnance Field Parks. Combat troops in every sense of the word, they embarked with the Commando, the Marines and the Infantry who were first to "touch down" first on Hitler's western wall. The Ordnance units which were selected to play their part in these gallant operations included the following, although some, in fact, did not land till several days after the actual assault.

Those which did land early supported our fighting men by giving splendid service :—

ORDNANCE BEACH DETACHMENTS :
   Nos. 7, 9, 10, 11, 12, 14, 15 and 36.

ORDNANCE AMMUNITION COMPANIES :
   Nos. 43, 44 and 45.

PORT ORDNANCE DETACHMENTS :
  Nos. 34, 35, 36 and 44.
PORT AMMUNITION DETACHMENTS :
  Nos. 34, 35, 36, 37, 38 and 44.
DIVISIONAL ORDNANCE FIELD PARKS :
  Detachments of the three Bde, Secs of 50 Division.
  3 British Division Ordnance Field Park.
CORPS ORDNANCE FIELD PARKS :
  Detachments of 1 and 30 Corps Ordnance Field Parks.
ORDNANCE MAINTENANCE COMPANIES :
  Stores and Ammunition Sections of 1 Ordnance Maintenance Company, with detachments of the Canadian Ordnance Maintenance Company 30 Armoured Brigade Ordnance Field Park.

Second Army Appreciation

Finally, before reviewing the actual events of D-day, what was the detailed Second Army Ordnance plan ? Army Group had delegated to Second Army the initial assault, and it therefore fell to Brigadier T. H. Clarke, D.D.O.S., Second Army, to prepare an "Appreciation of the Situation" covering the landing operations.

All the long months of careful planning finally crystallised in this historic document, which might be called the Ordnance "charter" for the invasion. Brigadier Clarke's Ordnance installations in Second Army had full responsibility for maintaining the Force from D-day till D+17, by which date it was planned that 21 Army Group would resume direct control. The assault and build-up stages were consequently an immediate Second Army concern, and Brigadier Clarke, in his Appreciation, had to consider the ways and means of achieving what proved to be a threefold target :—

  (a) to maintain with Stores and Ammunition Second Army, which would consist at this time of four Corps and attached Army, L of C and G.H.Q. troops, from D-day until D+17.

  (b) to handle unaccompanied Unit War Equipment ; and finally

  (c) to handle also the Signal Officer in Chief's reserves, medical stores of Ordnance origin and certain Civil Affairs stores.

Stated thus, very little impression is conveyed of the difficulty of the task which lay before Ordnance. Forming a background to all the planning done, and the foresight shown, there was always the element of hazard and uncertainty which surrounds an invasion from the sea of a strip of strongly defended land, together with the unpredictable tides and currents which arise in every battle, and no less important than any of these, the over-riding influence of the weather on every stage of the landing and build-up operations. This last was perhaps the most tortuous difficulty of all because, if the weather broke and our shipping programme was foiled, the Army would be starved of stores and equipment which, it was known, would be required in a steadily increasing stream, once we obtained a foothold on the Continent. It is against this background that the Appreciation of the Situation, prepared by D.D.O.S., Second Army, must be seen. Plans were made by him to meet every foreseeable contingency, and all the necessary physical preparations were completed to schedule.

D-Day Anticipations

The plan developed by D.D.O.S. Second Army assumed that on D-day and D+1 the Assault Formations would "live" on landing reserves and ammunition brought in under their own arrangements, e.g., the Ordnance Beach Detachments affiliated to the assaulting formations would ensure that the immediately required stores and ammunition were available. An additional Ammunition Company was placed under the command of the Assault Corps to assist in this early commitment. Similarly, Divisions landing on D-day and immediately thereafter were responsible for their Divisional Ordnance Field Parks, and Corps for their Corps Field Parks, including reserve guns and vehicles.

The object was to land between D+2 and D+8 sufficient "landing reserves" to maintain all Formations landing up to D+12 with first line stores, on the assumption that each landing reserve would last fifteen days for a brigade at intense rates. *In actual fact, between D+2 and D+8 sufficient landing reserves were landed to maintain all formations landed up to D+12 with first line stores.*

Subsequent to D+8, the Appreciation laid down that "Landing Reserves and Beach Maintenance Packs would be sent to 17 Advanced Ordnance Depot, to be consolidated with the special Advanced Ordnance Depot Packs." *On D+9 approximately, Beach Maintenance Packs commenced landing and were diverted to 17 Advanced Ordnance Depot.*

In the Appreciation and plan it had been decided that from D+5 the Beach Maintenance Area would be formed into two L of C terminals. No. 1 L of C Terminal would be under the technical control of A.D.O.S. Army Troops and No. 2 Terminal area would become the L of C Terminal. *On D+5 the Beach Maintenance Area was, in fact, merged into an L of C Terminal under the technical control of A.D.O.S. Army Troops.*

"On D+7," stated the Appreciation, "a second L of C Terminal will be formed." *On D+7 the second L of C was, in fact, formed, and the detailed arrangements foreshadowed in the Appreciation for dealing with Ordnance Stores there were fulfilled to the letter.*

In the Appreciation it was stated that "17 Advanced Ordnance Depot should not be expected to make issues until D+17."

Certain issues, mainly in the form of complete Packs to O.B.D's, were actually made from D+14 onwards, but full-scale issue did not commence till D+26. This delay was due to the serious storm which raged from 18-23 June, so that by D+23 less than 20,000 tons of the planned 40,000 tons of stores had been landed.

The Broad Plan

Broadly speaking, then, the plan was for the various Ordnance Beach Detachments—assisted by Ordnance Ammunition Companies and Ammunition Secs of 1 Ordnance Maintenance Company and Ordnance Field Parks—to maintain the Force with stores and ammunition for the first fortnight of operations. After this critical period, it was expected that they would be able to replenish their stocks from the Advanced Ordnance and Base Ammunition Depots which by then would be receiving stores. The Advanced Ordnance Depot did not open on the date fixed, due to circumstances outside its control, although it did make odd issues of complete packs to Ordnance Beach Detachments and Ordnance Field Parks from time to time during its "stocking-up" period.

Pending the setting up of the Advanced Ordnance Depot, it had been agreed in the Appreciation that unaccompanied G.1098 Euipment arriving before D+8 should be stacked in the nearest Ordnance Beach Detachment to which it landed; after that date it was to be consigned to 17 Advanced Ordnance Depot and 1 Ordnance Maintenance Company. This plan was followed without difficulty. Similarly, in the case of reserve vehicles, they were to be driven direct to the Advanced Ordnance Depot's Vehicle Parks. This, again, was the plan followed in practice.

In general, the steps laid down in the Second Army Appreciation of the Situation and briefing notes were followed almost to the letter, an indication of the soundness of the planning which had preceded the mounting of "Operation Overlord." The day by day time-table was adhered to with only minor amendments, brought about by the operational situation and change in the weather.

Ordnance Beach Detachments, Ordnance Field Parks, Port Ammunition Detachments, Port Ordnance Detachments and Ordnance Ammunition Companies, embarked according to the Staff Tables which had been worked out meticulously so many weeks in advance. The Bridgehead was gained, a lodgement made, stores began to flow across the beaches, our assault troops fanned out and extended their grip of enemy territory, the Beach Sub Areas came gradually into being, the Ordnance stores and ammunition "dumps" moved steadily forward from the beach area and the fighting troops were maintained by a continuous flow of stores and ammunition.

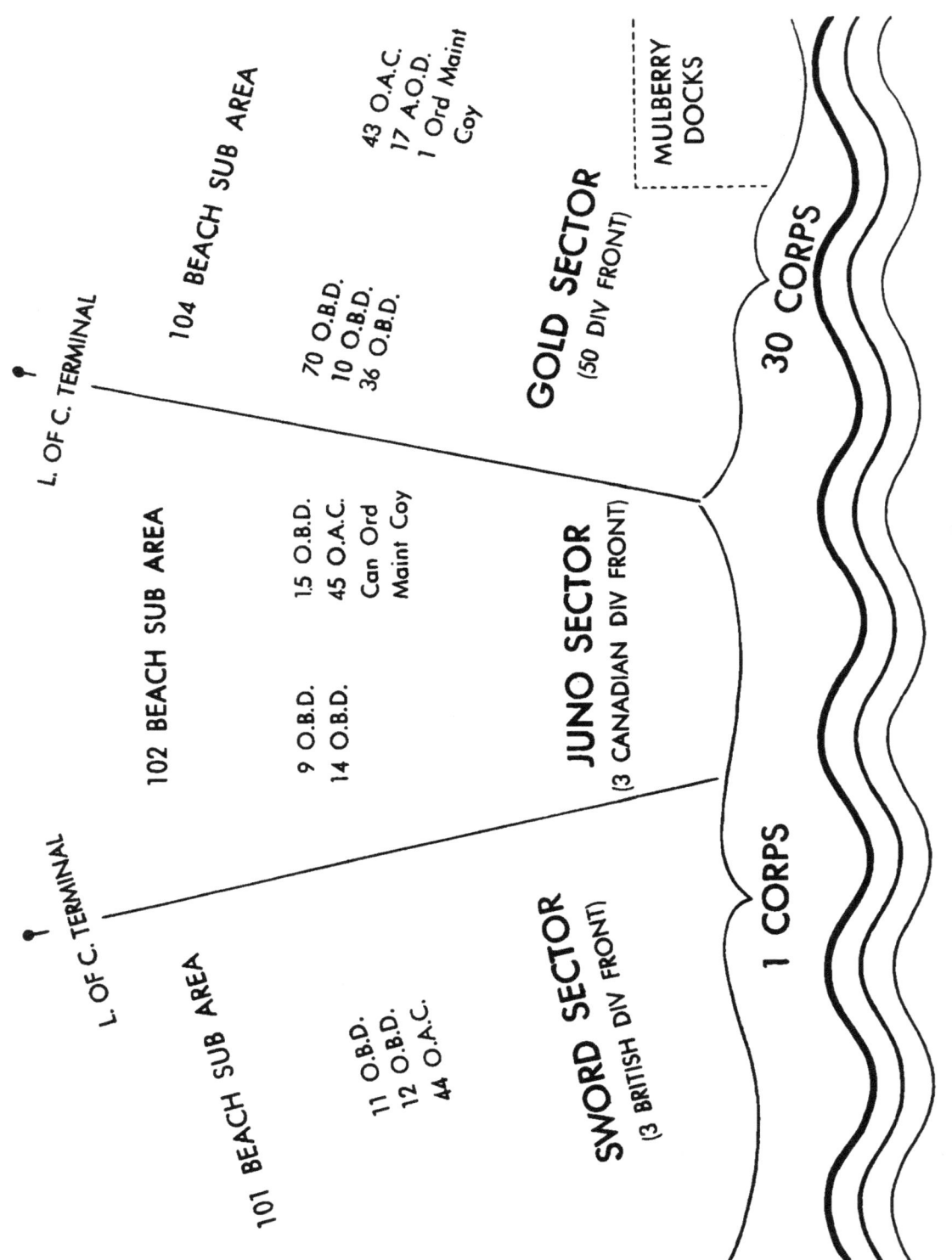

Chart of the Invasion Beaches

CHAPTER III

THE DAWN OF D-DAY

THE Landing on the coast of Normandy in the early hours of 6th June, 1944, was undoubtedly the most complicated and difficult invasion operation that has ever been made in history.

It involved such manifold consideration as tides, winds, waves, visibility in the air, visibility at sea, precision-timing and the combined deployment of tremendous forces fighting simultaneously on land, at sea and in the air. Even so, the operation as a whole was so accurately conceived and phased that considerable tactical surprise was effected—a most remarkable feat, having regard for the long forewarning which the enemy must have had of our intentions.

When information came to the Ordnance Directorate at 21 Army Group, some hours before the first blow was struck, that General Eisenhower had given the word to go ahead, there was complete confidence that everything possible had been done. Now, indeed, came the worst part of the whole experience of preparation. The D.O.S. and his subordinates had to wait, in suspense, for news while the world a large (fortunately, including Germany) slept blissfully ignorant of the tremendous events which were impending.

Very soon, their cheerful anticipations were justified by the arrival through Second Army of "situation reports" from Ordnance units with the two Corps which had been allotted the task of breaching the enemy's fortress; later from liaison officers specially sent over. These reports confirmed that the RAOC personnel who had landed were already making the great contribution expected. No less heartening was the information that casualties were light—much lighter than anticipated.

The first units to land were the Ordnance Beach Detachments and Ammunition Companies. Advance parties began to come ashore within an hour or so of the first assault troops. They immediately set to work, creating, "sector dumps" a few yards off the beaches in the footholds which the infantry had obtained. The main stocks were anti-tank and anti-aircraft ammunition, and in addition to Landing Reserves, stretchers and blankets for casualties, and also "survivors' kits," which later were in use for the first time. They consisted of kitbags containing a complete outfit of clothing, web equipment, rations, etc.—indeed, everything a soldier needed to put him back into battle if he were unlucky enough to experience a bad landing.

Formation of the Beach Sub Areas

Reference to the chart on the page facing will show how the invasion beaches were organised from the Ordnance point of view. In all, there were three Beach Sub Areas—101, 102 and 104. No. 101 Beach Sub Area was known as the "Sword Sector" and here the Third British Division made their assault over "Roger" and "Queen" beaches.

No. 102 Beach Sub-Area (or "Juno Sector") developed out of the "Nan" and "Mike" Beaches, which lay in the centre of the invasion strip, and here the Third Canadian Division made their landing. The two beach sub areas mentioned, therefore, fed the two assault Divisions thrown in by 1 Corps.

Away to the West, in an area which developed into 104 Beach Sub Area (or "Gold Sector"), 30 Corps effected a penetration, with 50 British Division mounting the assault. It was in this sector that the famous Mulberry Docks were constructed.

All beachheads were "strafed," but that in the East—101 Beach Sub Area, where 11 and 12 Ordnance Beach Detachments and 44 Ordnance Ammunition Company were operating—was shelled heavily from the Orne and had to be closed for a time under this withering attack. Notwithstanding this, Ordnance Stores were received into alternative sites, and the maintenance of the Force proceeded smoothly, despite this delay.

In the centre Beach Sub Area, 9, 14 and 15 Ordnance Beach Detachments, 45 Ordnance Ammunition Company and a detachment of the Canadian Ordnance Maintenance Company were deployed to support the Third Canadian Division. "Gold Sector," which lay west, was the avenue of direct approach to the ground earmarked for the Advanced Ordnance Depot and Vehicle Parks. Before these came in, however, valiant work was performed in this bridgehead by 7, 10 and 36 Ordnance Beach Detachments, 43 Ordnance Ammunition Company and 1 British Ordnance Maintenance Company, working in support of the assault made by 50 Division.

An insight into the phasing-in of Ordnance units operating on the beaches on D-day may be gained from the report on "Operation Overlord" prepared by one of the Beach Sub Areas. Due mainly to the bad weather encountered on June 5–6, the landing of Ordnance units did not take place exactly at the time forecast in the Staff Tables—there was a delay of about two or three hours. Furthermore, recce. parties which had been assigned the task of surveying sites for more Advanced Dumps, had to wait until first light on D+1, because the forward troops had not cleared the enemy from these positions.

First Dumps Formed on the Beaches

Since the ground in which the Beach Sub Area Ordnance dumps were to be set up could not be captured in time for these Depots to receive stores on D-day, initial dump areas had to be formed immediately behind some of the beaches. As might be expected, the space available in these temporary dumping areas was highly congested. Moreover, they were all under enemy fire until D+1.

The Ordnance Stores Depot for the Beach Sub Area consisted of two Ordnance Beach Detachment Stores Sections with an initial capacity of 100 per cent by D+2. The area allotted in the first Key Plan proved to be satisfactory, although owing to the stubborn enemy resistance encountered at this point, it was not possible to set up properly until about 12 hours after the time scheduled.

In this same Beach Sub Area, three Depots had been planned to receive 4,000 tons of ammunition by the evening of D+1, so that issues could be started by midday on D+2. The bad weather delayed receipts, but by the evening of D+2, both Ordnance stores and ammunition were flowing in strongly and work was proceeding smoothly.

On D+4, Ordnance stores in the initial dumps were cleared to the main Beach Maintenance Area Depot, and on D+5 ammunition which had been stacked in the initial dump was successfully cleared to the Beach Maintenance Area ammunition dump.

By D+6 the Second Army Roadhead was opened up at Bayeux where, in a matter of days, 17 Advanced Ordnance Depot began to receive stores in bulk. However, all this, and subsequent achievements, could not have happened as they did had not the Ordnance units disembarking on D-day done their job according to plan.

D-day Adventures

This phrase, "according to plan," has often been used to describe these early Ordnance achievements. But it would be wrong to suggest that urgent and sometimes inspired improvisation was not very frequently necessary to stave off almost certain delay or disaster. In this the little units, called upon to perform such prodigious tasks on D-day and after, shone brilliantly and often. Let us sketch the anticipated deployment of Nos. 11 and 12 Ordnance Beach Detachments, and No. 44 Ordnance Ammunition Company, as given in the briefing prior to D-day, and then compare it with the tactical situation which actually developed. Theirs is not a singular story, but typical of many.

11 Ordnance Beach Detachment and half of 44 Ordnance Ammunition Company were to play a part in the very first operations in 101 Beach Sub Area (see plan). They were scheduled to land on the first tide (at Lion-sur-Mer) and set up four Sector Stores Dumps in the gardens of villas about fifty yards off the beach. They had to be ready to issue

ammunition by H hour+240 minutes. In this interval, they had to make good their landing, ferry their ammunition across the beach, clear the gardens of the mines with which they were certain to be infested, and assemble their stacks; not bad going under enemy fire! Four landing craft (tank) were loaded with ammunition: e.g. one for each Sector Stores Dump. The first two were to touch down at H+120, the remaining two at H+240 minutes.

Meanwhile, at H+4 hours, a recce party from 12 Ordnance Beach Detachment were to land and recce the main dump site. This was at a point about a mile inland, south-west of Hermanville. The balance of 12 Ordnance Beach Detachment and 44 Ordnance Ammunition Company were to land between H+12 and H+16 hours and move directly to this main dump site. It was planned that ammunition would be received there from H+16 hours, by which time receipts into the temporary Sector Stores Dumps would stop. Issues from this main dump were to begin from H+24 hours, when the advance elements which had been operating the Sector Stores Dumps would come forward as reinforcements.

This was the plan. The breakdown shown above involved the splitting-up of the Ordnance Ammunition Company into nine different craft loads, and the two Ordnance Beach Detachments in a similar manner. This entailed careful planning, so that at all their eggs were not carried in one basket. Thus, had any one of the craft failed to touch down, it would not have materially affected the issue. Initial stores, such as signs, mine-clearance gear and a certain amount of stationery, were manhandled ashore in 10-cwt. trailers for the Sector Stores Dump.

Marshalling began on 28 May and was completed by 1 June. The Ordnance Ammunition Company was split into nine craft serials, in four of these with corresponding parties from 11 Ordnance Beach Detachment. On 30 May the first serials had embarked, and by midnight on 4 June, the whole Company was aboard its various craft. Early in the morning of 5 June, the first craft serials put to sea, knowing that at last it was the "real thing."

A D-Day Journey

The journey across was uneventful; the four parties in L.C.Ts (landing craft tanks) did not have a particularly comfortable time, as each craft carried 200 tons of ammunition, 20 tons of RE stores, five 3-ton lorries with an anti-tank platoon, a medical jeep and about 35 troops. Cooking had to be confined to the most elementary operations, such as brewing tea and opening tins of bully beef, carried out at the risk of a thorough wetting between the water-tight doors and the landing ramp. However, in view of the corkscrew motion of the craft, few people were interested in food!

There were no signs of enemy activity until the early hours of D-day, when the craft lay-to in sight of the French coast, and watched the Navy give a good pounding to the shore defences, and the assault troops go in under a heavy smoke-screen.

On moving inshore, they came under shellfire about a mile offshore, and this continued to be moderate, although surprisingly ineffective, until they were clear of the beaches.

Two landing craft, bearing the Officers commanding 11 Ordnance Beach Detachment, 44 Ordnance Ammunition Company and the Officer commanding the Ammunition Section of 11 Ordnance Beach Detachment, with 13 Other Ranks in each party, touched down on Queen "White" and Queen "Red" Beaches at H+120 minutes. The beaches presented a fairly chaotic sight, since the exits were jammed with tanks and it was impossible to move a vehicle. As mortar and light machine-gun fire from snipers was now added to the shellfire, and it was impossible to get off the beaches, they dug in at the back of the beach to await further instructions. The most heartening feature of the hour which they spent patiently waiting to get off the beach was the effective method of dealing with snipers in the houses on the sea-front—105 mm self-propelled guns firing into them at fifty yards range!

At about H+180 minutes, the parties linked up and got off the beaches, splitting up again and moving off to the first two Sector Stores Dumps. Just off the beach their first casualty occurred, when a Bren Carrier ran over a mine, the blast seriously wounding one man and shaking up several others. The Sector Stores Dumps sites were readily identified, and mine clearance began. In one Sector Stores Dumps, which was in the garden of a large villa, some twenty Teller-mines were found, in a patch of about 40 yards square, in the first half hour: about one in five of these were booby-trapped and had to be pulled. The Headquarters of 11

Ordnance Beach Detachment and 44 Ordnance Ammunition Company were set up at this Sector Stores Dump, and the first ammunition was received by DUKWS at approximately H+270 minutes. At about this time, a third Sector Stores Dump, set up along the concrete roads of an unfinished housing estate, came under heavy mortar fire from the direction of Colleville-sur-Orne, and several Pioneers were wounded. Fortunately, the enemy's shellfire was now passing over their heads and landing on the beach or at sea. The snipers, however, continued to be active, but were more annoying than dangerous.

When the second wave of L.C.Ts touched down at H+240 minutes, the first two Sector Stores Dumps were nearly cleared of mines, and the parties from these craft were sent to open the two remaining Sector Stores Dumps. One of the landing craft then received a direct hit in the engine-room and had to be abandoned. By this time ammunition was coming in fairly fast and the first units were beginning to come back for replenishments—particularly for 105 mm self-propelled guns, which were deployed on a line about half a mile forward and were using ammunition at a great rate.

The rest of D-day was comparatively uneventful. Personnel worked the first 48 hours without rest of any short, and amply repaid the training that had been given them.

Enemy aircraft made spasmodic efforts to get through and bomb the beaches, but were either blasted out of the sky by the Navy's intense A.A.-fire, or, if they survived that, caught by the Spitfires. It was a most cheering sight on the morning of D+1, when eight enemy aircraft came out of the clouds, to see five of them shot down immediately by A.A. and the remaining three within the next few minutes by the R.A.F.

Second Tide Parties

The second tide parties began to land during the evening of D-day. They met, however, with much worse weather than the assault parties, and had in many cases to abandon equipment and swim ashore. A sergeant of 12 Ordnance Beach Detachment was drowned in this way.

By the time they arrived, it was obvious that the original plan of deployment could not be followed. Fighting was still going in on Lion-sur-Mer and Luc-sur-Mer, a mile away to their right; there were still many enemy troops in the woods and orchards around Hermanville, and there was apparently strong fighting around the ridge Plumetot-Cressorons-Colleville, known as "Iceland" ridge. It thus became necessary to cram more ammunition into the already over-stacked Sector Store Dumps, and greater areas than were allotted to them had to be taken over. By extensive mine clearing and the use of a bulldozer or two, this extension was achieved, and issues and receipts continued to be heavy. During the first few days the depots were never empty of vehicles. Finally, some 3,000 tons were packed into areas for which 800 tons were originally scheduled. Safety distances were, of course, completely ignored—the 400 yards or so between the Sector Stores Dumps being the only safeguard. It was thought that the risks taken were justifiable—there were neither the men nor the time to clear a space for a normal type of dump, even had the opportunity occured.

Snipers continued to be troublesome, not so much in themselves, but in view of the vicious and concentrated fire they brought from the Navy. The "trigger-conscious" 20 mm gunners, deprived of the chance of shooting at enemy aircraft, were only too glad to open fire at the slightest suspicion of movement in the houses on the sea-front. Most of these houses were heavily booby-trapped and had not been cleared of snipers. They were afterwards found to contain a "rabbit-warren" of tunnels, in which the snipers hid. As the ground rose rapidly for a few feet on the landward side of the houses, 20 mm fired at snipers in the upper windows, usually went clean through the houses and passed over the Sector Stores Dumps at about eye-level. This was apt to be disconcerting! Once or twice the grass was set on fire, but fortunately was extinguished before any ammunition was affected.

On the morning of D+2 occurred the first really serious fire. Naturally, since the depots (which by now should have been scattered over the Beach Maintenance Area) were still within a few yards of the beaches, there was much congestion. One Sector Stores Dump found their small housing estate—perhaps 300 yards square—shared by an Ordnance Stores Dump, a Petrol,

L.S.T. Sails on D-Day

Oil and Lubricants Dump, an RASC Dump and the Army Post Office ! A chance Focke Wolfe 190, with one lucky bomb, hit the RASC Depot, causing waves of burning petrol to surge through to the Sector Stores Dump. Within thirty seconds there was a really good fire, which destroyed half the stacks of the Sector Stores Dump—about 450 tons—before burning itself out. In the absence of major fire fighting equipment, little could be done except to try and prevent the conflagration spreading, and some very fine work was performed, notably by Captain Thompson of 11 Ordnance Beach Detachment, Sjt. McGowan of 44 Ordnance Ammunition Company (awarded George Medal) and Sjt. Alden, also of 44 Ordnance Ammunition Company. These, together with a number of other Ordnance personnel and Pioneers, showed great courage and determination, actually breaking down burning 105 mm stacks with their hands, to prevent the spread of fire. Unhappily, Capt. Thompson was killed by a bursting 105 mm shell in the closing stages of the fire. During the height of the fire, 105 mm were exploding at the rate of about 10 per minute, and an area about 200 yards deep all round the Sector Stores Dumps was being swept by shell splinters. It is indeed surprising that there were not more casualties out of the hundred or so men engaged in fighting the fire, which lasted for about six hours. A fifth Sector Stores Dump was set up during the fire, to take further receipts. This came under heavy fire from Ouistreham and had to be abandoned later.

During the evening and night of D+3 the main dump was set up, the enemy having been cleared from both Luc and Lion. On D+4, during a fairly heavy air-raid, and in the middle of a very effective smoke screen, the Sector Stores Dump staff moved up to the main dump, leaving a skeleton staff to make urgent issues from the Sector Stores Dump.

Enemy air activity began to be a little more bold, especially at dawn and dusk, and on the morning of D+5 the Officer Commanding and a warrant officer of 44 Ordnance Ammunition Company were literally hunted from stack to stack, while making a stock check, by a Ju 88 which flew so low that the 40 mm. guns protecting the Depot could not be depressed to engage it!

On D+6 the area was bombed at dusk with "butterfly bombs," which set on fire a stack of 20 mm. and several stacks of 105 mm. There were three major casualties. Fortunately, there were adequate supplies of water available, and the fires were kept from spreading. Three stacks of 105 mm. and one of 20 mm. were lost. The bombing lasted over two hours and excellent work in collecting wounded and dressing them was performed under difficult conditions.

Stores Sections' Adventures

The foregoing covers the experiences of ammunition personnel. Similar adventures befell the Ordnances Beach Detachment Stores Sections who landed on the same beach (101 Beach Sub Area). For example 11 Ordnance Beach Detachment had the task of setting up four Sector Stores Dumps in the initial phase, in addition to other roles. In the early afternoon of D—1, the L.C.T.s sailed from England and had, fortunately, a quite uneventful trip across the Channel. Final briefing of the personnel took place during the voyage.

On approaching the coast of Normandy, they were sustained to see the heavy bombardments which the Navy was putting in. At "H-Hour," however, their craft ran into shelling from the enemy and, when they came within 700 yards of the beach, mortar fire also became intense.

One of the landing craft was hit, causing fire in the engine room, which necessitated flooding. Their second landing craft was also set on fire and personnel had to abandon ship. The ammunition, however, was saved.

The third craft, having survived a series of "very near misses," broke her back on beaching, as a result of detonating a mine.

On landing, all personnel faced intense machine-gun, shell and mortar fire. Owing to the large number of British tanks still on the beach, they were unable to off-load the vehicles containing their anti-tank guns until some 45 minutes after beaching. The O.R. personnel took cover in hastily dug slit-trenches near the beach exits, while the Ordnance Beach Detachment Officers went forward to "recce" the Sector Stores Dumps sites. This task took about 15 minutes and, in the meanwhile, the Ordnance Beach Detachment personnel had left their cover to fill-in the deep trenches caused by tank tracks and so reduce the danger of other vehicles being bogged in the soft sand.

Arriving at the first dump location, they found it still under mortar fire and also heavily mined. The sappers were unable to clear this particular site, so, without further delay, the two Ordnance Beach Detachment mine-clearing teams set to work with their own mine detectors, while the rest of the Ordnance Beach Detachment personnel used their bayonets as mine-prodders. In this way, altogether 80 mines were cleared in an area of approximately 150 square yards!

Combatant Training Justified

While these events were happening, similar action was being taken in the other Beach Sub Areas by the Ordnance Units which had landed. The wisdom of the combatant training during the months preceding D-day was now fully proved, and many RAOC personnel were complimented on the energy with which their sites were cleared, both of mines, booby-traps and other enemy impedimenta, and of snipers and small enemy reserves who had been by-passed by the assault troops.

CHAPTER IV

THE CAMPAIGN UNFOLDS—NORMANDY TO ANTWERP

A lodgement had been made in Normandy. Enemy counter-attacks had failed. Stores were now flowing swiftly through the pipelines which the R.A.O.C. had established. But all was fluid, changing from day to day.

Between D-day and D+5, as our forward troops battled their way on towards Caen, where the enemy had concentrated his main defences, Ordnance units were moving inshore and establishing larger dumps some miles inland. Landing reserves and ammunition were being handled by six Ordnance Beach Detachments, augmented by three Ordnance Ammunition Companies. Three main dumps had been formed in the three main sectors—Gold, Juno and Sword.

From day to day, Recce Parties were arriving to prepare the way for other Ordnance units. On D+2 and D+3, Recce parties from 17 Base Ammunition Depot, 1 Ordnance Maintenance Company and 1 Canadian Ordnance Company were landed. One important Recce party, unhappily, never reached shore. This was the all-important party from 17 Advanced Ordnance Depot, which was to be the first major stores Depot to supply the whole Force. The craft on which this party travelled was torpedoed in mid-Channel and all the senior Officers, with the exception only of the C.O.O. himself, were tragically lost. Casualties included the D.C.O.O., the O.C. Vehicle Companies, the O.C. Depot Battalion and the Officers commanding each of the three main sub-depots into which the Advanced Ordnance Depot was divided. This was a grievous blow, but others immediately stepped into the breach, and the Depot functioned with great success despite this early disaster.

The headquarters of 17 Base Ammunition Depot opened in the Juno sector on D+6 and exercised control over the three beach sector ammunition dumps, which were now working to capacity. 17 Vehicle Company, with reserve vehicles, started to arrive in the theatre on D+7. Beach Maintenance Packs of stores began to be received on D+8: this was the initial stock for 17 Advanced Ordnance Depot. The tonnage handled by this depot between 15 June and 30 June was approximately 20,000—an average of 1,300 tons a day. 15 Base Ammunition Depot opened on D+14. 12 Base Ammunition Depot landed on D+18. Ammunition brought over the beaches averaged 7,000 tons a day.

Withdrawal of Ordnance Beach Detachments

Events were now moving fast. The beach heads had been absorbed by the "Beach Sub Areas" and the latter were now melting into the bigger Beach Maintenance Area, which was soon crammed tight with men, ammunition, stores and equipment.

Up till D+5, the D.D.O.S., Second Army had delegated direct control of Ordnance units in the theatre to his two Deputies with the assault Corps. On D+5, however, the lodgement having been secured, HQ Second Army became directly responsible for the maintenance of the whole Force ashore. The Ordnance Beach Detachments in 101 and 102 Beach Sub Areas were now allotted for the maintenance of 1 Corps (No. 1 Terminal) and the Ordnance Beach Detachments in 104 Beach Sub Area were allotted for the maintenance of 30 Corps (No. 2 Terminal.).

On D+17 the receipt of stores in 101 and 102 Beach Sub Areas had virtually ceased, the flood now passing direct to 17 Advanced Ordnance Depot and 17 Base Ammunition Depot. Final disbandment of the Ordnance Beach Detachments made it possible to supplement the

Beach Maintenance Packs at 17 A.O.D.

personnel needed in increasing numbers for specialised tasks, such as tank-kitting sections for Corps, the staffing of Officers' Shops, etc. With the timely help of technical personnel, numbers of recovered weapons and wireless sets were repaired and issued, proving the importance of the early introduction of Returned Stores Depot facilities.

Clothing and Necessaries Important

It should not be thought that in these days of furious battle, all the excitement and urgency centred alone on warlike stores. On the contrary! When the tide of war sways to and fro, much depends upon morale. All things being equal, the side with the best morale wins. Morale has often decided victory in battle. It is that intangible something which every commander seeks, whose value no commander will decry. And Ordnance has a big part to play in the making of it.

If the soldier has not got a greatcoat to protect him from the cold, or a toothbrush to clean his teeth, if his boots want replacing, if he needs a change of underclothes or socks; if he has not the soap with which to wash himself—lacking these things, a soldier's morale suffers, however good is the supply of ammunition and warlike stores. That is why, from the very beginning of the campaign, the urgent supply of non-fighting, and to some extent superficially non-essential, stores was considered every bit as important as the flow of gun barrels, signal spares, and M.T. Clothing and necessaries were needed in immense quantities to maintain morale at a high pitch; and to the credit of the RAOC, morale did not suffer! In point of fact, the first two shortages which were the subject of urgent demands from the theatre were not, as might have been expected, guns, ammunition, tanks or any of the thousands of other warlike stores. They were for cotton drawers, and toothbrushes!

The First R.S.D. is Formed

By D+7 most of the personnel of No. 1 Ordnance Maintenance Company had arrived and they, in fact, proceeded to set up a Returned Stores Depot in the centre of the Bridgehead. This depot acted as a dump for captured enemy equipment, which was examined and, where necessary, packed and forwarded to the UK for detailed inspection. Unaccompanied G1098 equipment was also received, and units notified when to collect their essential war equipment.

This British Ordnance Maintenance Company was subsequently reinforced by a detachment from 1 Canadian Ordnance Maintenance Company, which later became responsible for the maintenance of the First Canadian Army at No. 1 Terminal.

Laundries and Bath Units arrive

Mobile Laundries and Bath Units were phased in as soon as possible, and lost no time in going into action. Apart from bathing troops, and washing hospital laundry, they assisted to a large extent in washing clothing and blankets recovered by the Returned Stores Depot, so that these items could be re-issued.

Industrial Gas Units and Base Hospital Laundries were soon following-up, doing valuable work in their respective roles.

By this time, too, great quantities of armoured fighting vehicles, personnel vehicles and load-carrying vehicles were being phased into the Vehicle Parks, and issued to Formations as replacements.

Arrival of 14 A.O.D.

14 Advanced Ordnance Depot, which had been earmarked as the main fully operative Ordnance Depot in the Rear Maintenance Area, commenced landing on D+23 and was located on D+54 in a site in Audrieu, which had been freed when the enemy retreated in the direction of Caen. The target date for the opening of 14 Advanced Ordnance Depot was D+90 and it actually opened on D+100. Consequently, initial depot stocks began to arrive almost as soon as the depot was planned.

In the meantime, 17 Advanced Ordnance Depot continued to maintain the force from landing reserves, beach maintenance packs and urgent stores consigned by Ordnance ships.

In order to anticipate shortages of vital items, a daily stock-state had been prepared by the Ordnance Beach Detachments in respect of fast-moving items. This was submitted to Second Army who demanded items urgently required. At 21 Army Group, it was arranged for an air-lift from the UK commencing on 22nd June, to supplement the intake of stores by express coaster.

Phasing the Advanced Ordnance Depot Issues

To ensure a fair distribution of the limited stocks during these early days, initiation of demands made on 17 Advanced Ordnance Depot by Ordnance Sub Parks and Workshops Stores Sections was fixed by Second Army at 50 per cent of the "maintenance figure." As the stocks increased, provision action was taken at 75 per cent of the maintenance figure and ultimately the normal maintenance figure was reached. A system of grading particularly urgent demands as "White Hot" or "Red Hot" according to priority, which had been decided in the UK, worked to the advantage of all, enabling the Depot to give preference to operationally important issues.

During the period of the advance up to the Seine, both British and Canadian Armies were maintained by road convoys from Ordnance Stores and Ammunition Depots to the Ordnance Maintenance Companies which functioned at Army Roadheads. An RAOC "Stores Convoy Unit," formed from 15 Forward Trailer Section, was also used to ferry forward stores of high operational urgency.

Problems of the Break-Through

The build-up of stores continued in the Rear Maintenance Area, but in anticipation of the break-through, 15 Advanced Ordnance Depot was brought into the theatre. Meanwhile, despite the saturation in the restricted bridgehead, there were certain compensating advantages. No L of C of any size had opened out. It was, therefore, possible for units to obtain urgent requirements of stores and ammunition within a few hours, according to the stocks in 17 Advanced Ordnance Depot, the Ordnance Beach Detachments and the Corps Field Parks.

So soon, however, as the break-out from the Normandy bridgehead was realised, and the Rear Maintenance Area thereby increased, Second Army roadhead was moved forward to the Falaise area. With the break-through, there was an immediate shortage of transport. This was to become more and more accentuated as the advance gained momentum and swept through France towards Belgium. Formations which had ordered hundreds of tons of stores whilst in the bridgehead, in order to build up adequate reserves, now leapt ahead without being able to accept them or indeed to carry them. Reserve vehicles were employed to the maximum on lifting stores forward. The transportation of urgently needed replacement stores, equipment and ammunition became as big a headache as their provision from the UK and their receipt over the beaches (where, with the exception of Mulberry "docks", there were still no proper port facilities).

Hours of work in Ordnance Depots were all the hours from dawn to dusk, and often through the night as well, for it became absolutely imperative that vehicles should not stand idle: if they were loaded with stores, they had to be emptied; if empty, they had to be filled. Prodigious efforts by the Pioneer and the Royal Army Service Corps helped to exact the maximum value out of this overworked transport. There was only one axiom: The Armies were clamouring for stores; they had to be satisfied.

21 Army Group Appreciation

An increment from 21 Army Group Ordnance Directorate had been attached to HQ L of C during the period it was responsible for operations. By this means it was possible to achieve a smooth take-over when direct responsibility for the Ordnance services in the theatre was resumed by the Ordnance Directorate of 21 Army Group on approximately 13th July. In preparation, the D.O.S. had prepared an Appreciation and also a Forecast of the situation expected by that date.

Position of Ordnance Field Parks at D+18

In this Appreciation it was foreseen that it would be a mistake to attempt to establish any form of Advanced Ordnance Stores Depot on the Seine. To do so would have meant opening a small depot furnished with an inadequate range of stores, or opening a depot stocked with "Beach Maintenance Packs" (which, in any case, could not be got ready in time by the home depots). The plan adopted was to rely on well-stocked Ordnance Field Parks, of which the following were under command:

1 Corps   *Portion ashore on D+18*

    1 Corps + Army Troops Sub Park   All
    103 Infantry Ordnance Sub Park   All
    203 Canadian Infantry Ordnance Sub Park   All
    151 Infantry Ordnance Sub Park   All
    3 Infantry Divisional Ordnance Field Park   All
    3 Canadian Infantry Divisional Ordnance Field Park   Part
    51 Infantry Divisional Ordnance Field Park   Part
    2 Canadian Armoured Brigade Ordnance Field Park   All
    27 Armoured Brigade Ordnance Field Park   All
    4 Armoured Brigade Ordnance Field Park   Part

8 Corps

    8 Corps and Army Troops Sub Park   Part (No. 1 Section complete)
    Guards Armoured Ordnance Sub Park   Part (No. 1 Section complete)
    111 Armoured Ordnance Sub Park   Part (Nos. 1 and 2 Secs complete)
    115 Infantry Ordnance Sub Park   Part (No. 1 Section complete)
    Guards Armoured Divisional Ordnance Field Park   Part
    11 Guards Armoured Divisional Ordnance Field Park Part
    15 Infantry Divisional Ordnance Field Park   Part
    31 Tank Brigade Ordnance Field Park   Part

12 Corps

    12 Corps and Army Troops Sub Park   Part (Nos. 1 and 2 Secs complete)
    143 Infantry Ordnance Sub Park   Part (Nos. 1 and 2 Secs complete)
    153 Infantry Ordnance Sub Park   Part (Nos. 1 and 2 Secs complete)
    159 Infantry Ordnance Sub Park   Part (Nos. 1 and 2 Secs complete)
    34 Tank Brigade Ordnance Field Park   All
    43 Infantry Divisional Ordnance   Part
    43 Infantry Divisional Ordnance Field Park   Part
    53 Infantry Divisional Ordnance Field Park   Part
    59 Infantry Divisional Ordnance Field Park   Part

30 Corps

    30 Corps and Army Troops Sub Park   All
    150 Infantry Ordnance Sub Park   All
    107 Armoured Ordnance Sub Park   All
    149 Infantry Ordnance Sub Park   Part
    50 Divisional Ordnance Field Park   All
    8 Armoured Brigade Ordnance Field Park   Part
    7 Armoured Divisional Ordnance Field Park   All
    33 Armoured Brigade Ordnance Field Park   —
    49 Divisional Ordnance Field Park   —

17 A.O.D. Gun Park near Vaux-Sur-Aure

In addition, the Armies had created Reserve "pools" of controlled stores which were with the Ordnance Maintenance Companies. Two Forward Trailer Sections were to be held as an emergency reserve holding, and Forward Maintenance Area packs of fast-moving clothing and general stores were to be fed forward regularly. Meanwhile, there was 15 Advanced Ordnance Depot in reserve, to form the nucleus of the advanced base, when a suitable port was captured. The holdings in the Army Vehicle Parks were to be increased and, as the L of C extended, they were to be echeloned forward in order to ensure the fastest possible delivery of operational replacement vehicles. Prior to the break-through, all Vehicle Parks were necessarily sited in the highly congested Rear Maintenance Area, where space was so limited that as many as three or four Parks were operating on the same location, although retaining their separate identity.

After the break-through was achieved, the Army Vehicle Parks accordingly moved up with their formations. Other Vehicle Parks were located at staging points along the L of C. The rapidity with which the Armies moved forward imposed a great strain on these Parks, and it was necessary to employ all available manpower, including reinforcements, to keep the advanced Parks filled for onward delivery to Armies.

It was decided to establish 3 Base Ammunition Depot at the Seine, with 17 Base Ammunition Depot free to leapfrog this point when the L of C justified it. A third Base Ammunition Depot still in the UK, was to be held in readiness for the final Advanced Base.

L of C Mobile Laundries were to be moved forward as the advance proceeded. No. 4 Base Hospital Laundry could move to the next medical area to be established, and No. 35 Base Hospital Laundry still in the UK was to be held for the final advanced base.

Again, in the case of the Industrial Gas Units, Nos. 31 and 32 Army Industrial Gas Units were to go forward with the Armies. Nos. 34 and 33 Army Industrial Gas Units were to be echeloned in the L of C. No. 1 Base Industrial Gas Unit was to be set up at Caen, while Nos. 2 and 3 Base Industrial Gas Units, still in the UK, were to be reserved for the next advanced base.

The location of the Advanced Base had not yet been fixed, but D.O.S. wisely kept a sufficient number of units of all types uncommitted to operations, so that, as and when a suitable port fell to our advancing forces, they could be switched immediately to establish this base and thereby reduce the ever-lengthening journey from the Rear Maintenance to the Forward Areas.

How the Plan Worked

The plan evolved by the 21 Army Group Directorate proved to be absolutely sound in conception, and as the pursuit sped across the French frontier and into Belgium, the D.O.S. was able to see the great port of Antwerp coming into view. Here his uncommitted Advanced Ordnance Depots, Base Ammunition Depots, etc., would be free to move direct, with the utmost expedition, and so open up the final Ordnance Advanced Base with the minimum of delay.

Quick decisions and urgent improvisations were necessary day by day to keep in step with the magificent sweep of our victorious Armies. With the crossing of the Seine and the rapid advance into Belgium, it became possible to consign stores forward by rail as far as the river Seine. Here, however, it was necessary to transport them by M.T. over the river, and then re-load on to the rail. Unfortunately this gave opportunity for a considerable amount of pilferage. Ordnance Railhead Detachments were sent forward to supervise the transfer of stores and ammunition at these points.

The distance which now separated the Armies from the Rear Maintenance Area necessitated the strengthening of stores-holding units in the Army Area. 15 Stores Transit Depot was moved forward to No. 6 Army Roadhead near Brussels to take over from No. 1 Ordnance Maintenance Company, which was moving forward as planned. Also, the projected forward movement of 17 Forward Trailer Section, with its emergency holding of important stores, was accomplished as foreseen, and the unit placed at the disposal of Second Army. A similar move on the part of 16 Forward Trailer Section, under command of the Canadian First Army, was made.

As the L of C stretched out to its utmost extreme, the strain on transport became so acute that only controlled stores and "white" and "red" hot maintenance could be guaranteed. Now a crisis arose in delivering the ordinary fast-moving clothing and general stores, and also spare parts for M.T., armaments, engineering and signal equipments. The historic advance had not been made without cost. Our Armies needed extensive re-equipping. Consequently, demands for Ordnance stores jumped alarmingly, both in respect of the quantity and the range of items requested.

With the rapid advance of roadheads, No. 1 Ordnance Maintenance Company became strung out in a series of small detachments all along the L of C and, as transport became available, it was used to bring the hindmost echelons forward.

As the Pas-de-Calais ports fell, ships bringing stock from the UK were diverted to them. 17 Stores Transit Depot was moved as soon as possible to Dieppe and later to Ostend. There was no point in continuing to phase UK receipts to 14 Advanced Ordnance Depot, which now lay hundreds of miles back in the Rear Maintenance Area. Antwerp had been captured, but the port was unworkable. 15 Advanced Ordnance Depot were there ready to stock up, and so, by using the ports of Dieppe and Ostend, 15,000 tons of initial stocks were shipped to this new Depot before the Antwerp port was opened. If this plan had not been adopted, the opening of 15 Advanced Ordnance Depot would have been seriously delayed, while the strain on the fast declining resources of 14 Advanced Ordnance Depot in the Rear Maintenance Area, and the transport needed to bring its issues forward, might have reached breaking point.

In step with the advance, the Ammunition Depots also moved forward in the direction of the ultimate Advanced Base. No. 3 Base Ammunition Depot was sent to Dieppe, to operate as the Advanced Ammunition Depot for the Canadian First Army. No. 2 Base Ammunition Depot went direct to Brussels. Then No. 3 Base Ammunition Depot moved from Dieppe to Ostend.

The Advanced Base at Antwerp was next occupied by 17 Base Ammunition Depot, which opened up there at the end of December. It was later joined by No. 15 Base Ammunition Depot, and also by No. 3 Field Ammunition Repair Factory.

Now, with the main stores and ammunition Depots operating at Antwerp, other units had gone forward again, so that the Ordnance organisation was at this stage spreadeagled over an area several hundred miles long. There were still a number of Ordnance units in the original Rear Maintenance Area, who were charged with the task of clearing their holdings forward to the new base. This involved the movement of hundreds of thousands of tons of stores and ammunition.

Tonnages Handled in the Advance

Between D-day and the end of February, the amount of stores and ammunition shipped into the theatre and handled in RAOC installations was :—

    ORDNANCE STORES :   418,634 tons.
    AMMUNITION :   825,693 tons.

During the same period, nearly 10,000 fighting vehicles, and over 53,000 non-fighting vehicles, had been received.

Issues of Ordnance stores averaged 1,000 tons a day. Issues of ammunition naturally fluctuated much more in accordance with the state of the battle, but Nos. 2 and 3 Base Ammunition Depots handled at times over 4,000 tons a day.

It was during this period of super-mobile warfare, when the whole front was on the move and each day brought a fresh expansion of the L of C, that Ordnance faced its severest test. However, the sound Ordnance planning which will be even more clearly seen in the chapters devoted to the Advanced Ordnance Depots and Base Ammunition Depots, enabled the Service to keep pace with all developments. It was backed by magnificent efforts on the part of all ranks in the field, as well as the unflagging support of War Office and the Central Ordnance Depots at home, who responded with alacrity to all requests made of them.

Due to this unfailing co-operation, the RAOC was, therefore, able to keep the British and Canadian Armies supplied with their greatest needs. The fighting soldier did not have to look over his shoulder for the maintenance he required in his heroic dash towards Germany.

CHAPTER V

THE STORY OF THE ADVANCED ORDNANCE DEPOTS

IT will be recalled that the Director of Ordnance Services had under his command four separate Advanced Ordnance Depots and that he had decided to make 17 A.O.D. the first main depot in the theatre. In view, however, of the size of the force, it was foreseen that one A.O.D. would be entirely inadequate to cope with the heavy receipts and issues of Beach Maintenance Packs, and therefore 16 A.O.D. was chosen to accompany 17 A.O.D. and the two units were temporarily merged.

The Recce Party of 17 A.O.D. embarked on 7 June 44 (D+1). It consisted of 16 Officers, including the Chief Ordnance Officer, Deputy Chief Ordnance Officer, Officer Commanding Vehicle Companies, Officer Commanding Depot Battalion, and the Ordnance Officers Commanding all Stores Companies, accompanied by 9 other ranks.

How easily planning and preparation can be foiled by a grave mischance of war was demonstrated by the fate which overtook their luckless craft. As previously disclosed, fifteen out of a party of sixteen A.O.D. officers, including those holding the major senior appointments, perished in this tragic incident. Thus, in one hard blow, had the main Ordnance Depot for the invasion lost all its most senior and experienced commanders, with the exception only of the C.O.O. himself—the very personnel who had planned in detail the whole organisation and layout and who, it seemed, would be quite irreplacable.

Arrival of 17 A.O.D.

A reserve Recce Party was immediately phased in, but did not arrive until the same date as the Advance Party (D+7). However, despite this early misfortune, the reconnaissance and preparation of the site were pushed ahead with the utmost vigour, and when the main party of the A.O.D. (who also were late in embarking owing to the intervening bad weather) arrived in the theatre on D+10, detailed sites had been agreed and arrangements made for the receipt of the intial A.O.D. stocks.

It was found that the areas allocated by Second Army in the First Key Plan were satisfactory, although the roads left much to be desired. Great assistance was, however, obtained from the Royal Engineers in developing old and in making new roads, and in general maintenance work. Nevertheless, the traffic circuit remained a continuous problem.

Defence measures were brought into operation smoothly and efficiently as a result of the intensive regimental training that had been undergone in England. Personnel were bivouaced, and no enemy activity was experienced during daylight, although throughout the hours of darkness enemy planes were constantly passing overhead and occasional machine-gunning on a small scale took place, with minor casualties.

Due to the bad weather, which had seriously delayed the shipping programme, the overall tonnage of stores received up to the end of June (D+24) totalled 19,139 tons, whereas the quantity scheduled was 39,240 tons.

The tonnage handled by this depot, having regard for the limited number of personnel available, is a record which testifies to the superhuman efforts which were made by the RAOC in the beachhead area. In the month of July alone, 17 A.O.D. received over 52,000 tons of Ordnance stores, and issued over 10,000 tons. In August, receipts had reached nearly 57,000

Wintry conditions at 14 A.O.D. Ps.o.W. in the background

tons, and issues nearly 23,000 tons. Thus, at a most critical time in the battle, when the enemy was striking back with all the strength he could summon, the British Second and the Canadian First Armies were kept richly supplied with vast quantities of essential Ordnance stores. The above figures do not take into account the considerable turnover achieved by the Returned Stores Depot, which had the task of clearing the bridgehead of Vote 7, 8 and 9 returned stores—a large quantity of which were taken back into the A.O.D. stock for re-issue.

It had been planned that 17 A.O.D. should commence issues about D+17, but in actual fact it was not found possible to reach this stage until the end of June, when a limited number of mechanical transport and technical stores issues were commenced. In the meanwhile, however, issues of complete packs had been made to assist Ordnance Beach Detachments and Ordnance Field Parks to maintain their role, and by the end of the first week in July, full scale issues from 17 A.O.D. had commenced. This depot continued to function until D+100 (14 September 1944), when the maintenance of the force was assumed by 14 A.O.D.

Role of 14 A.O.D.

Originally it had been intended that 14 A.O.D. would set up a semi-permanent Depot in the Caen area. This was the intention, but it could not be carried out because the enemy had consolidated his positions around Caen and we were facing a static phase in operations. Nevertheless, the formation of 14 A.O.D. could not be further delayed, since by D+100, 17 A.O.D. would have so exhausted its stocks that the percentage of availability from that stage onwards would diminish with increasing speed. Therefore, it became necessary to establish 14 A.O.D. in the only place available—short of Caen (where the existing buildings and roads would have proved a great advantage) in the open country. Eight potential sites were reconnoitred, the most suitable being Bretteville sur Odon. This last site would not be available for another three weeks, and already time was running short. The decision could not be postponed, but it was a hard choice which was left to the D.O.S. He had to decide (a) whether to wait a few weeks longer in order to build the new A.O.D. on the best site and thereby run the risk of 17 A.O.D. exhausting its stocks before 14 A.O.D. was ready to take over; or (b) start building at once on the next best site, which was on clay, accepting the assurance of the Engineer and Transportation services that it could be drained and made workable. The enemy's stubborn stand at Caen had already seriously delayed a start on the preparations for building 14 A.O.D., and the D.O.S. finally took the view that this urgent task could be deferred no longer. The risk had to be taken, and so the Engineers commenced work draining and constructing at Audrieu within 5,000 yards of the guns. But the weather rapidly deteriorated the hard core dissolved as fast as it was laid. Undismayed, the personnel of 14 A.O.D. worked in conditions which became increasingly difficult, and it is probable that no Ordnance depot of this size has ever had to perform so immense a task under such trying circumstances. The personnel were augmented by 15 A.O.D., by the arrival from 17 A.O.D. of the personnel of 16 A.O.D., by an increment equivalent to the Stores Companies of another A.O.D., and by large numbers of French civilians and German prisoners of war.

Yet another difficulty confronting 14 A.O.D. was the sudden unprecedented development of the L of C, following Field-Marshal Montgomery's break-through at Caen. For example, the Guards Armoured Division made an advance of 97 miles in 14 hours. It took them in one bound from Douai in France to the outskirts of Brussels. Stores soon had to be ferried forward along an L of C no less than 400 miles, but despite everything this depot continued to be the main theatre base of supply until the end of the year. During this long critical period, when so much was happening, the requirements of the force had expanded by the arrival in the theatre of the remainder of the build-up troops, and by further large drafts from the Main Base and overseas. The necessity of having a new A.O.D. sited well forward in the L of C near a Channel port, caused the D.O.S. to earmark Antwerp as the location of the next A.O.D. This was to be 15 A.O.D. who were gradually withdrawn from 14 A.O.D. and whose Recce-Party followed the spearhead of the Guards Armoured Division into Antwerp in the first week of September 1944, and began to seek accommodation, while the occupation of the docks was still under dispute.

15 A.O.D. Opens Up

They were able to requisition excellent storehouses and offices, ideally situated, with the improved road and rail communications that are usually available in a large town. These advantages had been denied the two initial A.O.D.'s, and they were soon to pay handsome dividends. A crowning asset was the employment of large numbers of civilian clerical and industrial staff who could both write and speak English fluently. With the almost unequalled port facilities immediately at hand, this new Advanced Base was, therefore, ideally situated to receive and issue stores to both the British and Canadian Armies, as well as units throughout the extensive L of C.

The new depot, which was to be of a more permanent character than either of its predecessors, was staffed initially by 15 A.O.D. This unit was quickly joined by the personnel of 17 A.O.D., the latter having now tidied-up their area in the Rear Maintenance Area. It was also proposed to absorb 16 A.O.D. personnel when issues ceased at 14 A.O.D., as well as the increment which had been sent from England to assist 14 A.O.D.

Once again the D.O.S. decided to retain one A.O.D. for any special emergency which might arise. Wisdom decreed that this should be 14 A.O.D., who, when they had finished making issues, could be employed in forwarding to the new Advanced Base such of their surplus stocks as were required there, and in generally clearing-up pending assigment to a new role.

For various reasons the port of Antwerp was not available for use in the first stages of the stocking-up of 15/17 A.O.D., as the new depot had been christened. A Stores Transit Depot was therefore deployed to handle intakes through Dieppe and Ostend, and the initial receipts from England arrived through these ports in the first week of November. At the same time, 14 A.O.D. also began to transfer stocks from the R.M.A., while maintaining their role as the issuing depot. Throughout the month of December, stores continued to arrive in increasing quantities, supplemented now by the opening of the port of Antwerp. In this month alone, 15/17 A.O.D. received 43,000 tons. A careful check on receipts enabled the A.O.D. to aim at the New Year as the date by which stocks should be sufficient to justify opening the depot for issues. This was, in fact, achieved according to plan, and by phasing the "take-over" into three easy stages, the load was absorbed smoothly and with complete success. On 1 January 1945, 15/17 A.O.D. began issues to the First Canadian Army; on 10 January 1945 to the Second British Army, and on 22 January 1945 to the whole vast L of C.

Size of 15/17 A.O.D.

How great was the importance of this new A.O.D. will be seen in the fact that by April— four months after opening— it was employing nearly 14,500 people. It then occupied three and a half million square feet of covered accommodation, and over thirty million square feet of open storage space (including Gun Parks) and its monthly turnover had reached 140,000 tons of stores. That this immense organisation was needed is proved by the fact that, whereas in January 1945, when the phasing-in of issues began, a total of 191,000 items were demanded of the depot, by March 1945 the figure had leapt to 469,000. A range of 126,000 separate items had to be stocked, provisioned and accounted. Availability reached and passed 80%.

In addition, greatly increased efforts were expended in the recovery of returned stores. In March alone, 21,000 tons of clothing, general and accommodation stores were handled by 17 Returned Stores Depot; over 13,000 tons of M.T., signals, wireless and armaments stores were handled in the same month by 15 Returned Stores Depot.

The policy of freely diluting military staff with English-speaking civilians proved an economic one. Of the total of 14,500 personnel employed, over 11,000 were civilians—the remainder were 2,471 RAOC and 1,053 Pioneers. This A.O.D. continued giving ever-improving service until the complete capitulation of the enemy, by which time D.O.S. decided that use should be made of the port of Hamburg. Accordingly, the C.O.O. of 15 Advanced Base Ordnance Depot (as the unit was now called) was charged with the responsibility of establishing a new Advanced

Ordnance Depot at Hannover and Hamburg to be provisioned, stocked and staffed by him, with the object of gradually superseding Antwerp and establishing Hannover and Hamburg as the new Advanced Base.

Second Role of 14 A.O.D.

Meantime, the D.O.S. still had available, uncommitted and ready for immediate deployment, 14 A.O.D., who had finished their work in the R.M.A. To this depot was given the task of acting as the principal "rundown" organisation through which, with the reduction of the British and Canadian forces in Germany, stores and equipment now surplus to their needs could be phased back to the United Kingdom for the Far-Eastern theatre. 14 A.O.D., therefore, became established at Hamburg, to carry out a large share of the "rundown" programme, while 15 Advanced Base Ordnance Depot in due course switched its base from Antwerp into the heart of Germany.

This, then, is the story of the Advanced Ordnance Depots. All of them functioned within shelling range of the enemy. 15/17 A.O.D., in particular, was under constant and heavy day and night air bombardment. The work was arduous, the hours long, the personal sacrifices many. But each depot, in its turn, put up a wonderful performance. The men who worked in these depots can feel justifiably proud of the part they played in smashing the Armies of the Hun. In the annals of the Royal Army Ordnance Corps, their achievments rank high.

CHAPTER VI

KEEPING THE ARMIES ON WHEELS

IN no previous war has transport played such a vital role as the one which opened in 1939. The armies of today swing into action on wheels: mechanical transport has endowed modern warfare with a speed and mobility never known before.

Upon Ordnance rests the responsibility first of supplying the necessary vehicles, and then of providing the spares which will keep those vehicles running. In 21 Army Group there were four Vehicle Companies charged with the first of these two important tasks.

Originally it was conceived that these Vehicle Companies, which respectively formed part of the Advanced Ordnance Depots, should work under the command of the Chief Ordnance Officer of their appropriate A.O.D. This was the plan followed in the early days. The Vehicle Companies of the combined 17 and 16 A.O.D. were deployed with the A.O.D. and formed an integral part of it. This arrangement worked well during the first phase of the invasion. The Vehicle Parks were sited close together in the narrow beachhead, and the C.O.O. of the Advanced Ordnance Depot was able to keep in close touch with them.

Separation of the Vehicle Companies

But when the break-through took place, this plan was no longer practicable. The stores side of the A.O.D. had to be expanded rapidly to supply the needs of the fast-growing force ashore. The Vehicle Parks had also to increase their holdings, and became widely dispersed all over the L of C.

So it was decided to bring together, under their own Chief Ordnance Officer, the Vehicle Companies of all four A.O.D.'s and to make him responsible for the supply of vehicles to the entire theatre. This happened on the closing of 17 A.O.D., and the combined Vehicle Companies ever afterwards remained a separate command. It was a sound move, for the turnover grew to four or five times the figure originally estimated.

But this anticipates our story. Once again it really begins with the planning stage in England when it was proposed to phase into the theatre, between D+2 and D+17, the first of the two Vehicle Companies forming part of the A.O.D. The second Vehicle Company was planned to come in from D+18 onwards. The recce party of the A.O.D. which, of course, included the vehicle element, was lost on the way over, and bad weather delayed the arrival of serials due in after D+17. Even so, the first reserve vehicle was issued on D+6.

How the Companies helped each other

Meanwhile, the Vehicle Companies still remaining in the UK also had a share in these initial operations. They assisted in water-proofing large numbers of vehicles, replacing vehicles found unfit in the assembly areas where units were concentrating, loading vehicles on landing craft, escorting them over sea, unloading them on beaches—and then returning to the UK for more! Consequently, all elements of the Vehicle Companies, whether or not their entrance as units into the theatre was late or early, helped to make possible the organisation which functioned so successfully in the original beachhead.

By D+25, a pier for vehicles had been constructed in Normandy, and drivers (who were not unused to "wet" landings) hailed this development with a sigh of relief! The famous Mulberry Docks was also occasionally used for vehicle off-loading. The waterproofing done in the

UK remained, nevertheless, a necessity since large numbers of vehicles still had to be driven off beached landing craft under their own steam. The intake, therefore, was influenced by the availability of berths and hards, the tides, the state of the weather, and the priority of other stores and equipment required to maintain the force.

The first Vehicle Company to land received all the reserve vehicles due in from D+2 to D+90. The second Vehicle Company was mainly used to drive the vehicles from the beaches to the Vehicle Parks. By D+60, however, two of the Vehicle Parks of this Company were also functioning—one as a detachment with Second Army, the other as a Park to supply units in the L of C. The third Company, which began to arrive from D+24 onward, was likewise initially used to ferry vehicles up from the beaches, while one of its Parks was detached to First Army. The fourth Company commenced arrival on D+80, and immediately assumed the ferrying role, thus freeing the third Company which was then regrouped to receive into its Parks the whole theatre intake. The second Vehicle Company, also by then relieved of its ferry duties, was lined-up likewise to assist the third in this big undertaking.

The Range of Vehicles

Thus the immense organisation for the receipt and issue of vehicles began gradually to take shape. Parks sprang up like mushrooms, initially in fields, side by side, along the Normandy roads, and later in echelon all the way to Hamburg! The number and variety of vehicles handled were impressive—in these Parks there were no fewer than 700 different makes and types. They ranged from a parachutist's folding motor-cycle to a tank-transporter 70 feet long! They included different types of armoured cars, bridge-layers, flame-throwing tanks, mobile cranes, surgeries, telephone exchanges, printing-shops, pigeons-vans, office-lorries, bulldozers, etc. The average stock grew to the neighbourhood of 45,000, and required 150 miles of hard standing.

The last-mentioned was, as may be imagined, extremely difficult to find. It did not exist at all in Normandy. Vehicles were parked in fields fed by narrow, crumbling roads. The maintenance of these roads was always the anxious concern of the Vehicle Park commander, and despite great help from the Engineers, he had time and again to fall back on his own resources for materials and labour. The bad weather experienced in Normandy played havoc with ground and road, and the heavy traffic in receipts and issues could not have been maintained without the strictest track discipline and a continuous plan for road maintenance. Specialist RAOC "Road Maintenance Teams" were eventually formed, recruited largely from prisoners of war.

Vehicles continued to be received water-proofed until about D+60. "De-waterproofing" was a task which occupied large numbers of personnel. With the capture of the Pas de Calais ports, better landing facilities became available, the intake through the Normandy beach-head was curtailed, and water-proofing abandoned. 15 Transit Vehicle Park was immediately brought up to exploit Ostend, and 17 Transit Vehicle Park to deal with receipts through Boulogne. Other Parks in the congested Rear Maintenance Area were now spaced out along the L of C. But every new vehicle supplied helped to make the war still more mobile! Vehicle Parks at Army Roadheads were sometimes sited and then evacuated inside the space of a few days or weeks, so fast was the thrust forward.

Even so, there remained some 9,000 reserve vehicles of various types still parked in the Rear Maintenance Area, now 300—400 miles behind. The turnround from Rear to Forward areas grew longer as the L of C lengthened, and more and more drivers were needed for ferry duties. The arrival of No. 1 Canadian Vehicle Company from the UK went far to alleviate this shortage.

Opening-up the Advanced Base

Now Antwerp was in sight as the new Advanced Base, and the Vehicle organisation looked forward to the day when this port could be used—for at Boulogne, Calais and Ostend "hards" were still being used to receive vehicles off-loaded from landing craft. Antwerp port would give a great fillip to the rate of discharging ships, and the long journey forward would be shortened. Vehicle Parks accordingly moved to new sites in the Advanced Base and along the main routes

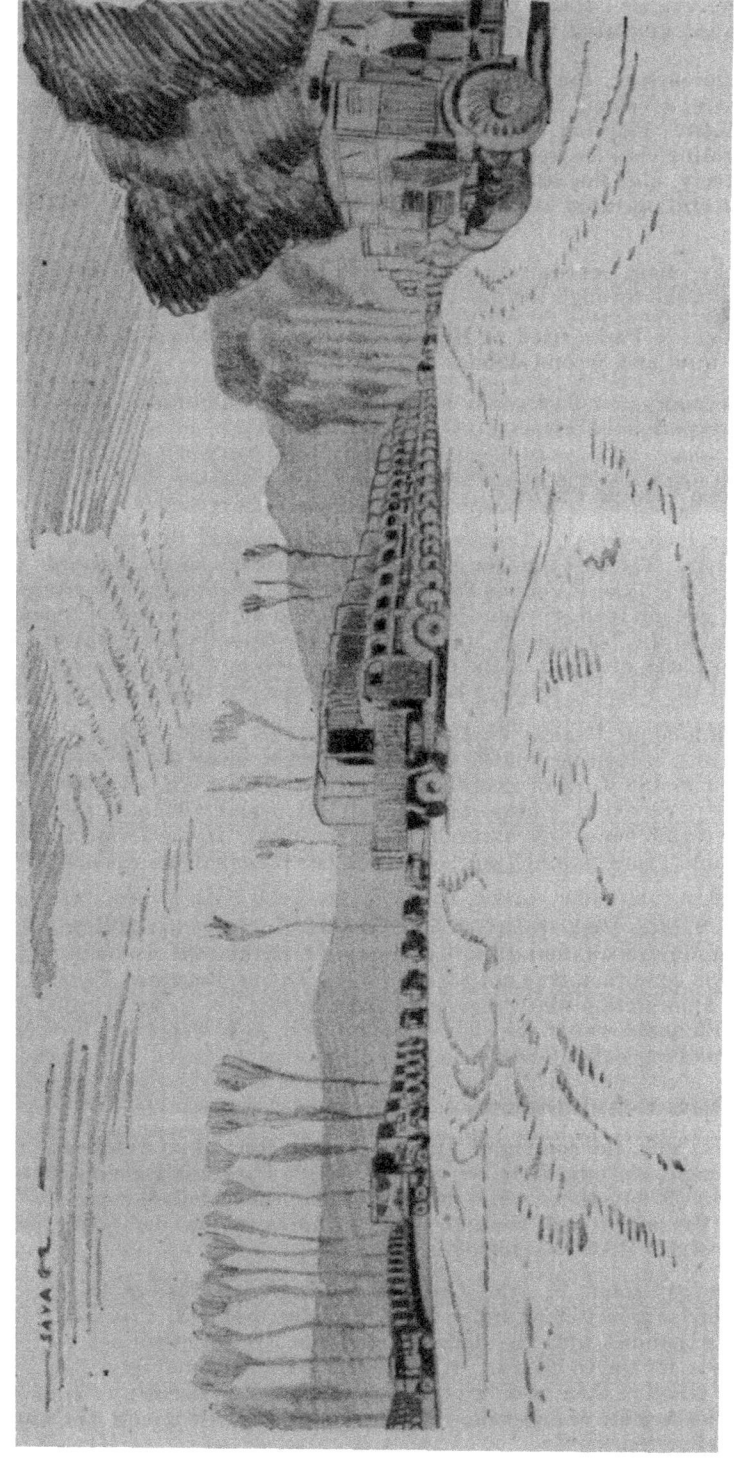

A Park of 17 Vehicle Company, near Vaux-Sur-Aure

forward to the Army Vehicle Parks. The flow of vehicles through Antwerp to these more forward-sited Parks continued unabated till the sudden collapse of Germany checked reinforcements.

As VE-day approached, the Vehicle Companies were spreadeagled over four European countries. In France, a Vehicle Park sited at Marseilles, was engaged in receiving vehicles sent from the Middle East. Fighting vehicles were consigned by train to Parks in the Advanced Base, while non-fighting vehicles went by road. Two Returned Vehicle Parks remained at Caen and Arras respectively, and the issue here depended on the rate of the recovery programme. Other detachments still operated at Calais and Boulogne for receiving and backloading certain types of vehicles.

In Belgium, the main concentration of Vehicle Parks remained in the Antwerp-Brussels area, handling the intake through the main port.

In Holland, Vehicle Parks sited at Nijmegen and Venlo enabled rapid replacement issues to be made to the First and Second Armies.

Finally, in Germany new Parks were coming into being and ultimately these were to cater entirely for the Occupational Force.

Organisation of the Vehicle Parks

And the Parks themselves ? Transit Vehicle Parks existed to "process" vehicles newly received in the theatre. The best time for initial maintenance is a soon as possible after discharging from the ship—so the Transit Vehicle Parks checked anti-freeze mixtures, batteries, oil-levels, tyre-pressures, and general road-worthiness as well as doing numerous minor repairs to put right small faults revealed in the "running-in" period or damage caused during transit. Additionally, the Transit Vehicle Parks disposed of the stores which were sent with vehicles to economise in shipping space, and the wheeled artillery and Radar equipment towed behind vehicles.

Separate stock-holding Vehicle Parks were formed to handle fighting and non-fighting vehicles. The "B" or non-fighting Vehicle Parks particularly made use of considerable numbers of civilians to assist in the work of maintenance and in driving convoys forward. Armoured fighting vehicles were received by transporters, by rail and, where distances were short, on their own tracks. Their maintenance was naturally more complex. In the severe winter, many were frozen into the ground ; turrets could not be turned, nor their hatches opened without running a flame round them !

The Returned Vehicle Parks received vehicles back from the battlefront. Sometimes half a ton or more of ammunition was found inside a damaged tank, and the removal of this ammunition, often in a dangerous condition, was not an easy task. In one Returned Vehicle Park, at least a thousand tons of ammunition were removed in the course of five to six months! Again, in these Parks, vehicle maintenance was of the highest importance, so as to prevent further deterioration and to preserve armament equipments.

VE-Day Brings New Commitments

As on the stores side, the coming of Victory saw the start of an extensive "rundown" programme. This brought an immediate increase in Vehicle Park holdings, owing to the disbandment of units. On VE-day there were roughly 45,000 vehicles in the various Vehicle Parks, but by VE+115, the stock had risen to 78,000 ! Meanwhile, demobilisation was making inroads into the available RAOC personnel.

Throughout the campaign, 21 Army Group was splendidly served by its Vehicle Companies. The turnover of vehicles grew to four or five times the figure originally expected. But the Vehicle Park organisation expanded with the demand, and the Armies continued to trundle forward at a rate too alarming for the Germans. In a war of unparalleled mobility, they kept the Armies moving. Had they failed in their task, we could not have got to Germany so quickly. But they did not fail, and the Armies of Liberation swept forward to victory on the wheels which the Vehicle Parks had provided them.

CHAPTER VII

PASS THE AMMUNITION!

A SOLDIER can fight without some equipment. But there is one thing without which he cannot fight; if it fails him, he is beaten. Ammunition he must have—plenty of it, too! And it must be where he needs it, and on time.

Between D-day and VE-day, nearly a million tons of ammunition were brought into the theatre and nearly three quarters of it were expended. Already in a previous chapter we have seen the exciting race which developed between the Ordnance dumps of ammunition and the troops who were consuming it. First there was the struggle to keep the assault Corps supplied on the beaches. Then there was the vast tonnage absorbed in achieving the break-through at Caen. Finally, when the Armies really swung into the offensive, there was the rush to keep our forward areas supplied over an ever-lengthening chain.

The first Base Ammunition Depot to arrive in the theatre was 17 B.A.D., followed quickly by 15 B.A.D. No. 1 Party of 17 B.A.D., which included the C.O.O., was scheduled to land on D+2, but eventually disembarked on D+4. No. 2 Party, embarking from Newhaven on D+2 in an L.C.I., touched down off "Jig" Beach opposite Le Hamel. They landed on D+3, in approximately 5 feet of water. The party proceeded to "Tennyson" transit area, and on the following day, marched to a point between Banville and Reviers, where they joined the C.O.O. and Party No. 1, and bivouaced for the night. Both these nights produced prolific sniping activity. No. 2 Party were assigned to 102 Base Sub Area. Here they joined up with 45 Ordnance Ammunition Company, which had been responsible for the organisation of the Beach Dump, and with the Ammunition Section of 15 Ordnance Beach Detachment. The first day was spent in "digging-in", as the enemy had shown themselves prone to using butterfly (anti-personnel) bombs and were becoming a little more bold in the use of their fighter and fighter-bomber aircraft.

On D+6 the party commenced work on the Beach Dump, which was known as 102 Beach Sub Area Ammunition Depot and was located approximately one mile inland from Courseulles, on either side of the Courseulles—Caen road.

The nights were made fantastically brilliant by the tremendous volume of A.A. fire which was maintained on the beach and from craft lying off shore.

Meanwhile, Party No. 3 had embarked on D+3 at Tilbury and sailed that night to contact the remainder of a convoy of some 400 vessels off Southend. The convoy then proceeded through the Straits of Dover, where intermittent enemy shelling from Cape Griz-Nez was encountered. Fortunately, our Air Force were in aggressive mood and succeeded in limiting this enemy activity.

Having run the gauntlet of the Straits, no further action was experienced until the convoy lay off the beach at Arromanches on the morning of D+6. Owing to overcrowding on the beach, it was not possible to land until approximately 1100 hours on D+7, one day and night having been spent at anchor. During this time, desultory enemy air attack was experienced. One of a small flight of German fighters was shot down into the sea near at hand by naval A.A. The mission of these planes was, presumably, to shoot up the multitude of assembled craft, which, had there been more enemy aircraft available, would have proved sitting targets. A battleship which was standing in the bay was employed in shelling the enemy inland, but lost no opportunity in assuming an offensive A.A. role when targets presented themselves.

The landing itself, which was made from an L.C.T. in approximately three feet six of water, was uneventful. On disembarking, the party marched to 102 Base Sub Area Ammunition Depot, to join the now well-established No. 2 Party who, with 45 Ordnance Ammunition Company and the O.B.D., were running this site.

Receipts, which had commenced on D-day, were at first spasmodic, being dependent upon the state of the tide. Transport at this stage was performed entirely by Dukws, and these vehicles were accorded a high priority. Irregularity of receipts from the beaches made it difficult to maintain an even flow of transport, but this was usually confined to early morning and due to first "flood" of Dukws already under load from the previous night.

Within a few days, standard types of lorries, mostly three-tonners, were being used to discharge beached vessels at low tide, but preference continued to be given to Dukws at all times.

Ammunition Dump Locations

The approximate areas allotted to the three Beach Sub Areas for ammunition storage were as follows :—

17 *Base Ammunition Depot* :

    101 *Beach Sub Area* : Lion-sur-Mer–Hermanville–Le Manoir–Cresserons.

    102 *Beach Sub Area* : Courseulles–Reviers–Beny-sur-Mer–to crossroads at the intersection of Bayeux/La Delivrande and Courseulles/Caen roads.

15 *Base Ammunition Depot* :

    104 *Beach Sub Area* : Ryes, through Sommervieu to the main Caen/Bayeux road, which it followed for approximately 3 miles, then following Seuller river to Le Manoir.

On D + 4, the C.O.O. had explored all three Beach Sub Area Ammunition Dumps in the hope of discovering possible expansion areas. This presented many problems, as owing to the restricted size of the beachhead, there was a multitude of all types of units stationed in and around the depot areas. Space was so confined that it was necessary to disregard all but the most elementary safety precautions in laying out the dumps.

On D + 12, No. 15 Base Ammunition Depot arrived. They commenced work at 104 Beach Sub Area Ammunition Dump, and now began to develop it into a full-scale depot.

Then, on D + 24, No. 12 Base Ammunition Depot arrived, and the Ammunition Companies forming this Base Ammunition Depot were temporarily placed under command of 17 and 15 Base Ammunition Depots. Later, as soon as another site in 104 Beach Sub Area was cleared, HQ personnel of 12 Base Ammunition Depot were withdrawn and began forming this further additional Base Ammunition Depot.

Meanwhile, personnel of 17 Base Ammunition Depot were engaged in operating 101 and 102 Beach Sub Area sites, thus making five ammunition depots in all.

Discharging Abandoned

The enemy had developed a disconcerting habit of shelling, from the direction of Le Havre, the ammunition storage areas at Lion-sur-Mer and Benieres. His efforts against the Lion-sur-Mer beachhead became so effective that discharging had to be discontinued on that beach for a period. The shelling of the Bernieres beach, however, did not seriously interfere with the discharging. About this time the Navy constructed a dummy beach head with derelict vehicles and landing craft and a genuine, but not too efficient, smoke screen—this had the desired effect of attracting some of the enemy's fire !

Enemy aircraft activity, which had been most persistent at night, declined rapidly towards the middle of July. Damage inflicted on the depots was slight in view of the number of aircraft which circled over them *en route* to the bay, where they were invariably met by withering fire from the craft assembled there. During daylight hours the enemy, by virtue of his lack of aircraft,

12 B.A.D. in Normandy

The first Base Laundry at Vaucelles

had confined his offensive activities to raids of the "tip and run" variety, but his losses on these missions soon became prohibitively high. The daylight raids ceased.

Bombs and sea-mines were, however, dropped at night on 17 B.A.D. Two sea-mines dropped one night on the Inspecting Ordnance Officer's Depot, succeeded only in wrecking several tents, in spite of the fact that they fell ten yards from stacks of anti-tank mines and demolitions.

One or two statistics are worthy of note concerning those precarious days, when it appeared to people working on the beachhead that the battle for Caen was interminable. During the period June 24th to June 30th, over 36,000 tons of ammunition were handled. Some issues were made by 3-ton lorry direct from the depots to the guns. Tactical loading was employed : e.g. on each lorry were loaded the exact number of shell, cartridge and fuzes, to make up complete rounds.

Issues and receipts continued by both day and by night without respite, and as many as 300 lorries were often handled during the three to four hours of full darkness.

The 5th of August produced the highest daily turnover yet attained, when 7,974 tons were handled in receipts and issues in 24 hours. These figures were eclipsed later at 10 Ammunition Roadhead during "Operation Plunder" (the crossing of the Rhine) when an all-time record was reached—9,150 tons of ammunition were handled on the 25th March, 1945.

For two days during the middle of June, weather placed a strangle-hold on receipts from the beaches. The wind, which reached and maintained gale force for almost 72 hours, precluded the discharge of ammunition to the Dukws from sea-going craft, and after several serious accidents, the unequal struggle was abandoned. The alternative of two practically ammunitionless days had to be accepted.

Big Explosion

On July 24th, an unfortunate explosion occurred at the Inspecting Ordnance Officer's Depot, where British mines, which had been lifted, were being returned by REs. It appeared that, in spite of a "safe to move" certificate, some mines were in an armed and highly dangerous condition. The result was that several thousand mines exploded *en masse*, killing three RE personnel instantaneously, wrecking two lorries and causing superficial damage to camps and personnel as far distant as one mile from the scene. Miraculously, no personnel of the Base Ammunition Depot received injuries of a serious nature, although several were working in the immediate vicinity. A Court of Inquiry, which was convened subsequently, found that no blame could be attached to either personnel or administration of the Base Ammunition Depot.

The I.O.O. Depot, particularly during July, received heavy consignments of returned British and captured enemy ammunition. Nor were these receipts confined to ammunition : small arms and other abandoned impedimenta also found their way into the "flow," to add to the difficulties of this depot.

On October 12th, for a period of five weeks, the I.O.O. was detached to 197 Infantry Brigade, which was engaged in battlefield clearance in the Falaise Gap. He became responsible for the clearance of both British and enemy ammunition, the latter being found abandoned in large quantities.

When enemy air activity subsided, a system of "street lighting" throughout the depot was evolved by REs, in order to render less difficult the recognition of ammunition boxes and the preparation of ammunition forms. November saw the closure of 17 B.A.D., when it moved forward and the remaining stocks were taken over by an indedendent Ordnance Ammunition Company.

The numerous small units which had rendered such valuable assistance during the days of tremendous tonnages, now rapidly moved forward, and the Base Ammunition Depot remained in virtual isolation. A programme of movement of ammunition by rail was commenced at mid-August, initially from Courseulles but latterly from Caen, which proved more satisfactory.

Weather conditions deteriorated badly in the autumn, and the movement of ammunition became very restricted. Throughout the latter part of September and the whole of October, it was necessary to employ caterpillar-track recovery vehicles, five of which were in constant use, to tow lorries from stacks to hard ground, where they could move under their own power.

During the 60-day period—D+13 to D+72—the two Base Ammunition Depots (17 and 15 B.A.D.'s), jointly handled 494,000 tons of ammunition (exclusive of internal movements and ammunition empties), giving a daily average of 8,230 tons in actual issues and receipts.

Our story has been chiefly of 17 B.A.D., since there is not the space to describe in detail the development of other Depots. Once their beachhead role was finished they were soon committed as heavily in the L of C.

Break-out from the Bridgehead

With the break-through achieved at last, considerable and swift changes were made in the chain of ammunition supply. A "cushion" area was opened in the Falaise area in mid-August, 1944, and an Ammunition Roadhead at Rugles by August 27th. This Roadhead was designed to hold 8,000 tons of ammunition.

Ammunition which the Corps had been unable to carry forward with them, was concentrated in a "cushion" area at Falaise. With the continued advance, a further "cushion" area was established near Arras in early September, but by this time the break-through had developed into a rout and Arras was never fully exploited. Instead, ammunition was lifted forward to the Brussels area. Next, an Ammunition Roadhead was opened near Bourg-Leopold. To feed the assault on the Rhine, a further Ammunition Roadhead was developed on the east bank of the river Maas, between Afferden and Arcen. During the stocking-up period, it was found that the supply of smoke generators was critical, and as a heavy smokescreen was needed for this operation, A.A. sites around Antwerp were combed to meet the exceptionally heavy demand. Altogether, 2,580 tons of smoke were eventually used for this operation!

By the end of March, the break-out from the Rhine bridgehead was achieved and once again, as previously in the sweep out of Normandy, Ordnance had to recce, stock and leap-frog one new dump after another, to keep pace with the advance of our victorious armies.

Ammunition Roadheads were established in swift succession at Metelen and Uchte. The demoralised enemy was now offering reduced resistance, and both Bremen and Hamburg were taken with a lower expenditure of ammunition than was expected. By VE-day, there were approximately 300,000 tons of ammunition in depots and dumps stretching from the Normandy beachhead right up to Lubeck.

Stores Section at No. 6 Army Roadhead at Enghien

A heavy "A" Vehicle Park

CHAPTER VIII

ON TO THE RHINE AND THE BALTIC

WE now leave the large, static installations to see how Ordnance functioned in the field. Already something has been told of the work done by these field units during the beachhead operations. But a better opportunity is afforded of seeing them in action by examining the campaign which opened after the capture of Antwerp.

The situation in September, 1944, was that the Second British Army, having invested this city, began to thrust north-east from the port in order to prepare for the Arnhem operation. The First Canadian Army took over the Antwerp area, and it therefore fell to the Canadians to clear the estuary and islands which barred access to the port. The Arnhem offensive was planned to take place on September 17th. The First and Third US Armies were assaulting the Siegfried Line. Now the stage was "all set" for the last thrilling act of the drama!

Second Army was to cross the Maas and the Rhine in the Grave-Nijmegen-Arnhem area. The purpose was to place Second Army in a suitable position for the subsequent development of operations towards the northern face of the Ruhr, in the great north German plains. The thrust to Arnhem outflanked the northern extension of the West Wall and came very near to success. From the start, however, adverse weather conditions prevailed and our airborne operations, which formed a vital part of the plan, were considerably curtailed and hampered. We gained much success but we were just not strong enough to force a decisive result.

The Ruhr lay before us, but we could not scoop it into our orbit.

And so a grim realisation dawned upon the Allies that their enemy was still far from beaten! It became plain that we should need to re-group and re-equip. Here, then, was another firm test of Ordnance, for the main flow of stores and ammunition was still from the Rear Maintenance Area, hundreds of miles away. Road transport simply did not exist in anything like sufficient quantity. The railways were only coming into operation, and were already over-taxed.

Throughout October the operation to clear the island and estuary approaches to Antwerp proceeded against bitter opposition, but by early November it was accomplished. Antwerp thus lay open to us at last. Very soon, its acquisition was paying handsome dividends. Ordnance stocks from the UK now came direct to Belgium, the new Advanced Base was rapidly hewn into shape, and the long and tedious "lift" from the Normandy depots became no longer necessary. Ordnance units felt the relief immediately and the re-equipment of 21 Army Group proceeded at a tremendous pace.

The Ardennes Break-Through

Then, in the midst of this build-up for the final bound into Germany came the Unexpected—von Rundstedt launched his famous drive through the Ardennes! Once more the weather had smiled upon the enemy, enabling him to spring his attack without forewarning, since for several days the Allied Air Force had been grounded. Rundstedt's main objective was Antwerp. If he got through, he could cut the Allied Armies and reduce their strategy to chaos. Field-Marshal Montgomery's quick and far-sighted counter-measures, associated with those of the American Armies, soon turned the tide, however, and Rundstedt was checked far from his goal, after having suffered enormous casualties.

Now, once again, we were given an opportunity to wrest the initiative from the enemy. Two operations were designed to secure this, and in both Ordnance had a key role. The first, under the code-word "Veritable," was to clear the Reichswald Forest and sweep up to the Rhine bank. The second, called "Plunder," involved the crossing of the river itself and an advance into the heart of Germany.

Even so, Rundstedt's offensive had upset our calculations. Battle wastage had to be made good: stores and equipments were needed to effect replacements. Nor was Field-Marshal Montgomery in mind to move before his Armies were completely re-equipped. Target dates were quickly set, and Ordnance representatives at all levels strove might and main to ensure that units were supplied to scale, and that the Field Parks—on which these units would draw after exhausting their own reserves—were stocked-up to the maximum.

Ordnance Planning for Operation "Veritable"

Over the whole battle area there lay a thick blanket of snow. It was, therefore, necessary for Ordnance to supply special snow and mountain equipment for an operation which might take place under arctic conditions. This meant providing stores and equipment which had not previously been wanted in the theatre: *e.g.* white smocks, necksquares and trousers for camouflage, snow goggles, sledges, ice-axes and windproof clothing. But this was only looking one step ahead! What would happen when the thaw set in? Much of this equipment would be an encumbrance then—so Ordnance had to lay in other no less specialised equipment which would enable our troops to adapt themselves to watery and muddy conditions.

In fact, the thaw *did* arrive—two days before the date set for the operation. This was bad enough, but the enemy, in anticipation of our attack, blew the Ruer dams and the whole battlefield was transformed into a muddy sea. The amphibious vehicles which the Ordnance Service had brought up now enabled the offensive to continue — Dukws, Weasels and other similar craft churned their way through the lakes which sepearated the "islands" of higher ground. The only supply road soon lay three feet under water. In this nightmare operation, the Ordnance Field Parks, Sub-Parks and Mobile Laundries and Bath Units of the following Formations took part:—

> 51 Highland Division;
> 53 Welch Division;
> 15 Scottish Division;
> 43 Wessex Division;
> Guards Armoured Division;
> 2 Canadian Division;
> 3 Canadian Division;
> 6 Guards Armoured Brigade;
> 8 Armoured Brigade;
> 34 Armoured Brigade;
> 11 Armoured Division;
> 30 Armoured Brigade (of 79 Armoured Division).

All these Formations operated under 30 Corps, so that the Deputy Director of Ordnance Services of this Corps had a very wide responsibility. The Corps in turn was responsible to First Army, to which all these British formations were temporarily attached.

15 Scottish Divisional Ordnance Field Park was brought up to Nijmegen, and supplied the assault force in the opening phase of the attack. The intention was to strike south-east from Nijmegen and clear the area between the Maas and the Rhine. 15 Scottish Divisional Field Park maintained this drive, and later as it developed south-east, the other Ordnance installations, which had not been moved up, were better placed to take up the maintenance role over a shorter line by ferrying supplies directly across the Mass. The south-east swing was strongly resisted at first by the enemy, and 15 Divisional Field Park at one time found itself obliged to maintain upwards of ten Divisions. During this phase of the operation, this unit actually achieved the remarkable record of issuing in full, 90 per cent of the demands made on it.

Despite the snow which handicapped preparations, the thaw which clogged them, and the flooding which bogged them, the service provided by the Ordnance units of the formations engaged in "Operation Veritable" somehow contrived to feed supplies forward, and the battle was won. Our troops moved up to line the Western bank of the Rhine, and then paused to re-equip for the next fight.

Getting Ready for the Rhine Crossing

The Rhine was the last great barrier. True, other rivers lay beyond, in Germany. But they did not present such obstacles, nor were they likely to be so stiffly held by the enemy, to whom "Father Rhine" had become something sacred. The crossing of this river was indeed a formidable task, and once more special stores were wanted for an offensive almost as big as the original operations on D-day. Just before the mounting of this offensive, the Commander A.R.G. inspected the tank forces assembled and had only two further requests to make of Ordnance. One was for white paint and the other was for mudguards, both of which were supplied.

An aspect of this preparation not usually appreciated is the amount of rehearsal required before mounting a difficult operation. 30 and 12 Corps were jointly charged to make the assault crossings. They therefore carried out a number of secret exercises, for which Ordnance had to provide equipments and stores so that the exercises could be conducted in a truly realistic fashion. As a result of these schemes, a suitable technique was evolved for the crossing of such a wide river as the Rhine.

Ordnance was then called upon to produce Asdic Echo-Sounding Apparatus, Fluorescent Tape and Panels, Light Floats, Land Mattresses, Tabby Equipments, Mae Wests, Weasels, Windsor Carriers, and other special equipment. Not only had these to be provided, but replacements and spares had to be brought up to the Field Parks. Operational reserves of normal land vehicles, guns and controlled stores had also to be amassed well forward. Survivors' kits were accumulated in the L.V.T. loading area. Reserves were required of flame-throwing and industrial gases. Further, as there was always the possibility that the enemy might resort to some desperate, last-minute, gesture, first-line reserves of anti-gas equipment and clothing had to be ready.

Ordnance Units in Operation "Plunder"

It will be seen that the planning of Operation "Plunder" represented a considerable effort. It was, therefore, with much satisfaction that the Ordnance Directorate received from the two Corps singled out for the assault, the assurance that all their deficiencies had been made good before their D-day arrived.

Among the 30 Corps Ordnance units which took part in Operation "Plunder" were the Field Parks, Sub-Parks, Laundries and Bath units attached to:—

> 51 Division ;
> 43 Division ;
> Guards Armoured Division ;
> 3 Canadian Division ;
> 8 Armoured Brigade ;
> 3 British Infantry Division ;

12 Corps, which was jointly responsible for the Rhine crossing, had the Ordnance units of the following Formations engaged :—

> 52 Lowland Division ;
> 15 Scottish Division, which carried out the assault on 12 Corps front ;
> 53 Welsh Division, which was charged to make the break-out with 7 British Armoured Division ;
> 7 Armoured Division ;
> 1 Commando Brigade ;
> 34 Armoured Brigade ;
> 4 Armoured Brigade ;
> 31 Armoured Brigade ;
> 115 Infantry Brigade.

Meanwhile, 8 Corps, with its various Ordnance services, lay well back from the river bank. This Corps was held behind until the bridgehead was established and was then to go through, completing its strength by picking-up formations on the East bank of the Rhine.

Eve of the Rhine Crossing

By the 20th of March, the concentration of troops began. The assault and Commando units of 30 and 12 Corps moved to their Marshalling Areas (shades of June, 1944!) At this time, camouflage stores were much in demand from Ordnance. The enemy had to be deceived at all costs as to the precise places where we intended to assault the river. A heavy smoke-screen was put down all along the Army Group front—again Ordnance was involved, and the provision of smoke generators in the quantity demanded imposed a heavy strain on ammunition dump resources. The screen was actually one of the biggest ever used in operations, and succeeded completely in confusing the enemy as to our ultimate intentions.

Finally, as D-day approached, forward reserves of stores, vehicles and equipments were concentrated close to the river bank ready to take across immediately the bridgehead was gained. It was the 6th of June all over again, even to the Navy taking part! The air force did its preliminary pounding of enemy communications concentration areas and defensive points an, and the troops of the Sixth Airborne Division—the same which had done the original Normandy landing —were ready to make their drop, in which, once again, the RAOC played its part.

H-hour for the operation was 2100 hours on the 23rd of March. Exactly at this time, as planned in the time-table, 30 Corps troops crossed the river on both sides of Rees. At 2200 hours, as planned, 1 Commando Brigade of 12 Corps made the assault, crossing the river about two miles west of Wesel. Early next morning at 0200 hours, again as planned, 15 Scottish Division made their assault crossing. We thus had several positions on the Eastern bank of the Rhine, and these were soon consolidated into a useful bridgehead.

Hard on the heels of the assault troops followed the forward stores holdings, and as soon as a bridge was available, Ordnance units supporting the various Formations were pouring across as fast as their wheels would carry them.

The maintenance of the 30 Corps spearhead fell to the Ordnance units of 51 Division while those with 43 Division and the Guards Armoured Division supplied the "build-up" force with stores.

Ordnance Services for the Break-out

Now began the magnificent drive of Second Army which was to thrust as far into Germany as its vehicles, stores and ammunition would take it. By D+4, 8 Corps had taken over 6 Airborne Division (which had landed north of Wesel) and had under command, with their appropriate Ordnance installations :—

> 11 Armoured Division;
> 1 Commando Brigade;
> 6 Airborne Division;

Later this Corps took over command:—

> 15 Division;
> 5 Division and
> 6 Guards Armoured Brigade.

The Divisional Field Parks, the Corps and Army Troops Sub-Parks and the Mobile Laundries and Bath units—even the Officers' Shop!—tailed on to the expedition. The Corps advanced at a rattling pace, so much so that every morning for several weeks the Ordnance HQ at Corps moved punctually to a new location! The office lorries were at their new site and in operation by 1100 hours each day, from which time work went on steadily till midnight, and often afterwards.

Advance Endangered by—Fan-belts

The maintenance of armour in the spearhead of an advance required very urgent decision and improvisation on the part of the Ordnance services of all three Corps. During this headlong rush to the Elbe, a typical instance occurred when the 8 Corps Commander telephoned one day to make a seemingly impossible request. In the winter, 11 Armoured Division had been equipped with a new secret tank, and now in the dash forward a serious fan-belt fault was revealed. The Corps Commander declared that unless he had 200 new fan-belts inside 48 hours, his Division would have to stop and the whole advance would be jeopardised. The fault had not been disclosed before and there were no replacement fan-belts in the theatre ! Energetic action by the D.D.O.S. of 8 Corps saved the situation. The fan-belts required were flown from England, rushed to the 11 Armoured Division Ordnance Field Park, and within 48 hours they were fitted to the tanks. The advance of 11 Armoured Division did *not* stop. It went crashing through, as hoped, to the Elbe.

In the confused situation which developed as a result of the cut and thrust of these dashing armoured spearheads, Ordnance recce parties often found themselves in close contact with the enemy. An instance occurred when the I.O.O. of 8 Corps was driving through Munster Forest on his way to take over an enemy ammunition dump which the forward troops had signalled. He was suddenly ambushed, dived out of his Jeep to take cover in a ditch and owed his life to the timely arrival of a platoon of 53 Division, who were engaged in clearing the wood.

Many interesting discoveries were made by Ordnance representatives *en route*. D.D.O.S. of 8 Corps found a factory engaged in production work for the German atomic bomb. The ammunition for Germany's largest gun was also located. Two of these massive guns had been captured by the Russians, but this was the first time their ammunition had been seen. At Belsen, the Ordnance service found itself faced with an unprecedented task. About 45,000 half-naked men, women and children were found in the Camp. Clothing could not be provided from Army stocks, but the necessary garments were obtained by a "levy" on surrounding German towns and villages. Clothing and accomodation stores in vast quantities were also improvised to meet the needs of the great numbers of released prisoners of war and displaced persons who were found in camps, or who had taken to the roads in their thousands.

The Break-up of German Resistance

It was in early March that the enemy had been hurled back from the Rhine all along the 21 Army Group front. This was the beginning of the end. Every new day brought an increasing tempo in the swift round-up of the fast-disintegrating German Army.

The pursuit of the enemy to the Baltic continued, soon surpassing all expectations. There was little opportunity for planning its maintenance, but nevertheless, planning had to take place. It was foreseen that should Second Army maintain the momentum of this advance, very soon it would be faced with the same crippling handicap which had menaced the supply of stores after the break-out in Normandy. Second Army was now investing a large tract of Germany, and the line from Antwerp might rapidly become as attenuated as the one which had formerly stretched back from Antwerp to the beachhead. It was known that, in these circumstances, the normal transport available for Ordnance stores would be quite inadequate to maintain the force. Plans were accordingly made in the midst of the battle to ground, by mid-April, the stocks of the Corps Ordnance Sub-Parks, Army Troops Ordnance Field Park and 17 Forward Trailer Section. All the vehicles and trailers thus released and, in addition, reserve vehicles from Second Army Vehicle Park, were merged to form "RAOC Transport Columns." In this way, the urgent operational needs of the spearheads were met. In many cases, too, operationally important stores were flown to them from the Advanced Base.

The momentum of the advance never faltered through lack of Ordnance supplies. One river line after another was assaulted and taken. Famous German cities fell like skittles before the relentless drive of Second Army. Meanwhile, the First Canadian Army was completing the "liquidation" of all the German forces in Holland.

By the end of April, it was plain that the fighting was almost over. The German Army was on its knees, and, sure enough, capitulation moves were already under way. Ultimately the

"Cease Fire" sounded all along 21 Army Group front at 0800 hours on the 5th of May. Through all these operations, the Corps and Army Troops Field and Sub-Parks, the Divisional Field Parks, the independent Brigade Sections and the Workshops Stores Sections gave consistently good service to their respective Formations. Typical was the output of 30 Corps and Army Troops Sub-Park, which was in action from Normandy forward. Between the 20th of June, 1944, and the 31st of May, 1945, this unit was asked altogether for 170,000 items, including those which it was not scaled to carry. It issued over 110,000!

These figures are the more commendable when the wide and difficult range of items furnished is remembered. In the armaments section alone, such a unit has to carry 6 pdr., 17 pdr., 25 pdr., 40 mm. (self-propelled and mobile), 3.7 A.A., 7.2 and 155 mm. Wireless sets include the various editions of Nos. 12, 18, 19, 22, 38, R 107, R 109 and Can. C. 9. The load-carrying problem was never easy to solve. Consider the stock which a Corps and Army Troops Sub-Park must carry in the shape of tyre covers and tubes alone! 12 Corps and Army Troops Sub-Park issued as many as 290 covers and 220 tubes in a single week.

Elasticity of the Field Parks

Not all the Field Parks operated in the manner laid down. Experience showed that local modifications could be introduced with improvement in the standard of service rendered for a particular role. The organisation of a normal Divisional Park provides for an HQ Section and three Brigade Sections. The HQ Section is scaled to serve divisional troops, and the Brigade Sections according to the holdings within the various Brigades. This allows a Brigade Section to be detached and to move forward independently with its Brigade, if required.

In the case of 43 Division, however, the Sections were re-scaled on the principle that one should issue M.T. stores, another wirless, signals and armament stores etc. Finally, one Section was left with its representative holding of all stores, except that stocks of controlled and specially rationed items were built up. This last section was re-christened the "Advanced Section" and operated independently of the rest of the Field Park, going forward to maintain the spearhead troops. It was, of course, smaller and therefore easier to move than a full-scale normal Divisional Field Park, and it provided such excellent service that in course of time the Division never moved without it.

The story of 43 Divisional Field Park illustrates the experience of the many similar units which participated in the campaign. First it supported its Division in the battle of Caen. Then began the long trek which so many units were destined to take, as the battle swept first across the Seine, then through the heart of France, then on into Belgium and Holland, and finally into Germany.

As this unit went forward through the liberated continent, never far behind the fighting troops, it passed hundreds of towns and villages where the local populations, thrilled with the ecstacy of their newly-won freedom, lined the streets to cheer and shout their exclamations of gratitude. All this time, the unit was issuing stores to maintain the Division on its onward march.

When the Field Park arrived at Nijmegen, the road was cut behind it. This, again, is an experience which has several times befallen forward Ordnance installations. In the battle to support the Arnhem drop, availability averaged 70 per cent, some days rising to 85 and 90 per cent. Issues from 43 Divisional Field Park averaged 4,000 items a week.

Problems of the Peace

The sounding of the "Cease Fire" on the 5th of May, 1945, on 21 Army Group front did not mean respite for Ordnance. The wholesale surrender of the German forces introduced new problems which required urgent action. Once again wastage had to be made good: units of all kinds were demanding replacement spares and equipments. A proud enemy had to be made sensible of the full extent of his defeat: Victory parades were mounted, which meant immediate and heavy demands for new battledress, headdress, boots, formation signs and flags of all the Allies! In over-running Germany, many dumps of ammunition and stores had been uncovered: Ordnance personnel had to take charge of these and sort out the materials which we could convert

Glimpses of an Ordnance Field Park

Forward Trailer Section near Bayeux

to our own use. Finally, victory meant a reduction of the British and Canadian Armies on the Continent : a run-down programme had to be devised to receive back the stores and equipments of disbanding formations.

Definitely the aftermath of victory was no picnic for the Ordnance Service of 21 Army Group. While the problems of the peace lacked the urgency known in war, they became every bit as complicated and far-reaching. It was found necessary to "freeze" the release of Ordnance Officers of early age groups. The re-organisation of the Corps to meet its new commitments fell to Major-General C. Cansdale, CBE, who was appointed Director of Ordnance Services for the Rhine Army. Brigadier L. E. Cutforth, OBE, remained Deputy Director of Ordnance Services, in which capacity he had served in the planning phase before the invasion of Europe and through all stages of the campaign.

Thus, within, a year of completing their preparations for the maintenance of the force to invade Normandy, Ordnance personnel of 21 Army Group were busily engaged in preparing the demobilisation of the same force. Still, they could look back on that year as one of boundless achievement. They had fully maintained the armies of liberation and so played a part in restoring freedom to the Continent and in banishing, let us hope ! for all time, the shadow of German aggression from the face of Europe.

CHAPTER IX

SPECIALIST ORDNANCE UNITS

Scene : The long, dusty road to Rheine.

Characters : An Infantry Battalion of 52 Division.

Time : March, 1945, during the advance into Germany.

Temperature : Described afterwards as "at boiling point."

THE Battalion has reached the outskirts of Rheine and its object is to occupy the town. Rounding a corner in the road, the spearhead is confronted by the sign :—

"35 M.L.B.U."

The tired and grimey Tommies rub their eyes. An Ordnance Mobile Laundry and Bath Unit *in front* of the Infantry ! Impossible ! True, the M.L. and B.Us usually keep well up with the fighting troops. They are the branch of Ordnance, best known, and certainly most popular, among all ranks.

The faces of these battle-worn veterans broke into broad smiles when they caught a glimpse of the showers, and realised they were not dreaming—there really was the chance of a bath here, and a change of clothing. What this means to the fighting soldier only those who have seen action can imagine. The Ordnance Laundry and Bath Unit is one of the best morale-boosters known to the modern army, and in the fighting in North-West Europe it has won wide admiration.

Of course it is not customary for a Baths Section to go ahead of the Infantry ! But it is certainly not unusual to find the showers in operation only a few thousand yards behind the front line. This time an enterprising officer had done an advance recce, found the Germans evacuating the near side of the town, and decided to rush up his Baths Section so as to stage a pleasant surprise for the Infantry spearhead. These men could now have a refreshing bath and receive fresh underclothing, shirts and socks in exchange for their soiled linen, which would later be washed and handed out to other troops. That is how a Mobile Laundry and Baths Section works, ensuring that men are kept clean in clothing and person, thereby maintaining health and personal cleanliness, even in the midst of battles. In a very real sense, the Mobile Laundry and Bath Unit is the most personalised side of Ordnance, and a well-run outfit not only does a grand job but is the best possible advertisement for the Corps.

The Mobile Laundry and Bath Unit can give every man in a Division a bath and change of clothing once a week. This is some turnover, but it represents only one phase of the laundry service evolved by Ordnance and operated so successfully in 21 Army Group. Five basic types of Laundries were used, Type "A" consisted of two boiler trailers, two washing machine trailers, two drying machine trailers and two generators. Type "B" was made up of four self-contained Laundry trailers, each trailer carrying boiler, generator, washing machine, dryer and dynamo. Type "C" was a mixture of the first two types.

Now we come to the larger units—the "Base Laundry," which is mobile, and the "Base Hospital Laundry" which is only semi-mobile. Type "D," which is the Base Laundry, consisted of six mobile equipments of "A" type. The Base Hospital Laundry (Type "E") had its machines mounted on platforms. The equipment of this unit consisted of a complete laundry including ironing machines, presses etc., and weighed about 250 tons.

Planning the Hospital Service

Naturally it was the hospital service which received prior attention in the laundry planning of "Overlord". The Ordnance Directorate at 21 Army Group were advised by the RAMC of the hospital phasing, and lined-up their laundry service to cater for these units. The medical plan was to have 3,000 beds in the theatre by D+17, building up to 40,000 by D+90. A complication which arose was that neither of the two main laundry types—the Base Laundry and the Base Hospital Laundry—could be shipped into the theatre before D+30, and it would take up to 30 days to erect their plant.

So it was decided that the smaller, mobile laundries would have to cater for the hospitals up to D+60. The plot was as follows:—

(a) *Up to D+16*, the Corps and Divisional Mobile Laundries would concentrate on hospital washing.

(b) *From D+16 to D+30*, three Army Troops and L of C Mobile Laundries would take over this work.

(c) *From D+30 onward*, the load would be progressively assumed by the Base Laundries and Base Hospital Laundries as they came into the theatre and got their plant going. No. 2 Base Hospital Laundry was soon dealing comfortably with 15,000 hospital beds, working two 8-hour shifts daily.

To begin with, therefore, the soldier was issued with soap and had to do his own washing. But when the Army Troops and L of C Mobile Laundries got into their stride with the Hospital work, the Corps and Divisional Mobile Laundries and Bath Units were freed to assume their normal role. Within a month of D-day, as a result of this careful planning, forward troops were having showers, and getting their clothing exchanged; the hospital washing was being handled efficiently; and shipping space, which was then so valuable, had been reserved for operational stores and not usurped by the heavy Hospital Laundry equipments. These came in from D+30 onward, as planned, when the beachhead was firm and the shipping space could be spared.

One month later (D+60) there were in the theatre three Base Hospital Laundries, one Base Laundry and *all* the Mobile Laundries and Bath Units required to service the force. 2 Base Hospital Laundry was the first of its type to function in the theatre.

These installations smoothly carried the growing hospital load, washed blankets received back from the Front in the Returned Stores Depot, and gave the Divisions a bath and clean clothing issue which was acclaimed by all units.

Consequences of the Break-Through

With the fall of Caen, a civilian laundry was taken over—the first of many to be used as the advance swept through France, Belgium, Holland and Germany. There were never enough Ordnance Laundries to cater for the extensive L of C in the early days, nor could sufficient civilian laundries be found in working condition. But with the liberation of Belgium, the needed civilian plant was uncovered; and as winter approached, L of C troops were given a full laundry service. Some 200 civilian laundries were soon engaged in this work, catering for both the military and RAF located in the L of C.

Meanwhile the forward laundries were doing a big job. With the development of civilian contracts in the L of C, several base installations were released to go right up the line. For example 34 Base Laundry moved to Eindhoven, where it came under air attack and suffered casualties. 4 Base Hospital Laundry moved to Ostend to serve the hospital area formed there. 2 Base Hospital Laundry moved to Brussels, while 35 Base Laundry moved to Antwerp. Shortly after, 34 Base Laundry was on the move again, this time to the Hannover area. No. 3 Base Hospital Laundry remained behind in Normandy and supervised various civilian contracts, in addition to running their own plant.

A Mobile Laundry Unit at Work

No. 1 Base Industrial Gas Unit

So much for the base installations. But all this time the Mobile Laundries and Bath Units were moving forward with their formations, keeping morale high and helping to stem infestation and disease. So far forward were these popular and hard-worked units that stories abound of the aggressive role sometimes forced upon them in action—the taking of German prisoners by M.L.B.U. personnel was a very common occurrence! Some of these sturdy little units used to crack the joke that the best showers were reserved for customers who undertook to escort one of their unwelcome guests *back* to the forward areas!

The Fight against Death at Belsen

Certainly the grimmest task which confronted the Mobile Laundries and Bath Units fell to the lot of those attached to Formations of 8 Corps, which uncovered Belsen. Before the liberation of this notorious concentration camp, intelligence reports had been received at Corps headquarters hinting at the conditions which they might expect to find there. Incredible as the information seemed, the Deputy Director of Ordnance Services, 8 Corps, thought it wise to have a Laundry and Bath Unit officer standing by, ready to send to the Camp immediately it was captured on April 15th. This officer was, therefore, one of the first arrivals in Belsen, where he was horrified to find that the advance information had not been exaggerated in the smallest detail. The Camp was a cess-pool of filth and disease; men, women and children were dying by the hundred every day; and 10,000 unburied bodies, in various stages of decomposition, lay around.

"Priority one" was to get the medical services going, and within 48 hours, 304 Mobile Laundry was in the Camp—and working. Bath Sections of 304, 106, 305 and 310 Mobile Laundries had arrived within a matter of days, and inmates of the Camp were soon having their first bath since imprisonment. These sections also assisted the hospital by providing hot water, and it was thrilling for the Ordnance personnel to see how the morale of the prisoners, who had been living for so long in indescribable filth and fear, quickly responded to the food, medical and sanitation services which their British liberators provided. It was obvious that the Bath Units played a big part in reviving morale. Even so, despite everything that could be done, the lives of many prisoners were beyond saving, and the death-roll continued to be heavy for many days. On arrival, these Ordnance units had found some 28,000 women and children, and about 17,000 men, in the Camp. All ranks worked day and night to stem the holocaust of dirt and infestation. Every day brought improvement, but it was an almost impossible task and eventually the worst sectors of the Camp had to be burnt down to stop the spread of disease.

The Largest Order Executed

The biggest single order which the Ordnance Laundry organisation had to face arose with the hand-in of winter clothing. In the spring of 1945, something like a million blankets were withdrawn, and every one of these had to be washed in readiness for re-issue in the Autumn! This was accomplished on time by exploiting the bulk of the bleaching and scouring machinery of the Belgian textile industry. The difficulties in obtaining sufficient coal and power for this tall order are best left to the imagination.

But the washing of a million blankets was a side-show as compared with the regular and personal service, afforded first to the hospitals and later to the whole force, by the Ordnance laundry and baths organisation. In a hard and gruelling campaign, this branch of the Corps won nothing but praise from all Arms and Services. It did not have an easy job. There were all sorts of difficulties in connection with machinery, movement, output, water, effluent, blackout etc. But they turned on the steam, literally, and worked to deserve the many fine compliments paid them.

Industrial Gas Units

The production of Industrial and Flame-thrower gases is an Ordnance responsibility, and as might be surmised, considerable quantities of these gases were required by 21 Army Group.

Till D+40 the whole theatre needs were met by shipments from the UK. This arrangement was made pending the arrival of Army Industrial Gas Units, four of which were brought into

Normandy between D+20 and D+40. Although their production could not supply the requirements of the whole force, they remained an invaluable emergency source of oxygen and acetylene. In addition to supplying industrial gases to workshops, they were also called upon to produce medical oxygen for hospitals.

With the capture of Caen, a useful civilian plant was acquired to supplement production. By the time Rouen fell, sufficient civilian apparatus was working to enable the theatre to become self-supporting. Small detachments of the Base Industrial Gas Units were dispersed to these centres to supervise production. Personnel from No. 1 Base Industrial Gas Unit operated civilian installations at Caen, Rouen and Lille; while sections from No. 3 Base Industrial Gas Unit were soon functioning at Brussels, Antwerp, Ghent and Breda.

A section of No. 3 Base Industrial Gas Unit had received training in the UK in the production of inert gas, which is a mixture of nitrogen and CO_2. This is employed as the propulsion agent for the inflammable liquid used in Crocodile and Wasp flame-throwing equipments. This unit arrived about D+18, but the demand so increased that a further detachment, with additional plant, had to be brought in shortly afterwards. Undoubtedly the production of gas for these secret weapons did help to shorten the war. Lifebuoy spheres, which form part of the personal flame-throwing equipment, were also filled.

One of the Base Industrial Gas Units suffered severe casualties when operating in the Antwerp zone. It received a direct hit from a "V2" rocket, every senior technical N.C.O. on the strength being killed.

With the climax of the war, demands for industrial gases remained high. Workshops still consumed large quantities in their recovery work.

An interesting project in which Ordnance assisted was the dismantling of Mulberry Docks and also certain of the German beach obstacles. Gases were produced for use by oxy-acetylene burners in cutting up sections for return to scrap-yards in the UK!

Forward Maintenance Stores and Ammunition Sections

The names of these units give a good idea of their role, which was well forward, maintaining the advance force.

As an example of how the Stores Sections were used, the case of 30 Corps is typical. This Corps took part in the original landing and the Rhine crossing. It had two of these units under command: 54 and 55 Forward Maintenance Stores Sections.

They were deployed by having one heavily committed and the other lightly loaded and mobile to "leap-frog" as and when a new thrust took place. They received the bulk consignments, broke down at Corps level into Formations, and were one of the last links in the chain of supply from Base.

Small, compact units, the F.M.S.S.'s and F.M.A.S.'s were always well "in the picture" of a battle, and rendered fine service.

Armoured Stores Company

Among the many Ordnance units which were privileged to see their work directly influence the trend of a battle, the Armoured Stores Company is a noteworthy example.

This Company specialised in tank equipment, and worked in close association with the Armoured Replacement Group of the Royal Armoured Corps. It had a section with the Army Delivery Squadron to check the kitting of tanks issued by them, and also detachments with each of the Corps Delivery Squadrons.

Tank warfare was always an outstanding feature of operations in this theatre and when the Armies broke out of Normandy, the immediate replacement of casualties suffered by our roving armoured spearheads became a matter of supreme importance. It directly affected the whole course of the war.

D.O.S. appointed an A.D.O.S. to work with the Armoured Replacement Group, and an Armoured Stores Company was formed under his control. He advised the Armoured Replacement Group Commander on all problems arising out of the equipment of armoured fighting vehicles and self-propelled guns. He was able to forecast the requirements of the Group, so that adequate Ordnance provision could be made; and by liaison between Army Group and the Advanced Ordnance Depot, he strove to ensure an even flow of fighting vehicles and equipment to meet the changing operational situation. It was no easy task, but it was done.

Between D-day and VE-day, over *eleven thousand* armoured fighting vehicles and self-propelled guns were kitted and issued, the Armoured Stores Company being responsible for checking that all these vehicles went out equipped in a battleworthy condition. Some 2,620 of the fighting vehicles had been received from Workshops, so that the amount of re-kitting necessary was substantial.

The range of tools and equipment required for an armoured fighting vehicle must be seen to be believed. Many of the items are "attractive" and pilfering resulted in considerable deficiencies which the Armoured Stores Company had to see made good. As may be imagined, once the Armies were on the move, the time available to do this kitting was fractional.

Anticipation was the key-note. Prior to the Maas and Rhine crossings the Ordnance Sections with Corps Delivery Squadrons were stocked-up to the limit. When these operations were mounted, and our armoured columns leapt forward, replacement kits were issued at such a pace that fresh tanks were invariably on their way within an hour of being signalled. In short, the Armoured Stores Company saw that replacement armoured fighting vehicles were issued with their full battle-scale of equipment. Thereby they helped to maintain the momentum of an advance which was to teach the German Army something new in blitzkrieg tactics!

Ordnance Maintenance Companies

Occasional reference has already been made to the Ordnance Maintenance Companies supporting both the First and Second Armies. Although sections from these Companies were assigned various emergency tasks, the main role of the units was to operate the Army Roadheads, which were always moving. Here they handled Ordnance stores coming up originally from Normandy and later from the advanced base at Antwerp. During the tremendous advance from the Seine, and also in the offensives in Holland and Germany, they were an essential link in the long supply chain, and handled thousands of tons of operational stores.

Forward Trailer Sections

The forward Trailer Sections were originally designed as a forward holding, on wheels, of operationally important Ordnance stores. Each of the four Advanced Ordnance Depots in 21 Army Group had one such section; but only two of the four Forward Trailer Sections functioned in the Forward Area. These were 16 Forward Trailer Section, which was attached to First Army; and 17 Forward Trailer Section, which went forward with Second Army.

Early in the planning stage it was realised that the Forward Trailer Sections could not carry a worthwhile scaling of everything. War Office had not provided tractors, and the trailers themselves were unsatisfactory, having a poor ground clearance and being very prone to flats. The deployment of the Forward Trailer Sections, therefore, became the subject of much discussion between the Ordnance Directorates at 21 Army Group and the War Office. In the end it was decided that 21 Army Group should have authority to use the units as it felt best, and the following plan was adopted:

14 FORWARD TRAILER SECTION

This unit was scaled to provide M.T. spares for the very big commitment of units in the L of C. Later A.A. scaling was added and 14 F.T.S. did yeoman service in screening the A.O.D. from a flood of small "detail" issues.

15 FORWARD TRAILER SECTION

This unit was scaled to cover three tank brigades. It was not used as planned, but was eventually re-scaled to cater for Army Base Workshops in the Antwerp area. Like 14 Forward Trailer Section, it provided another very valuable "screen" for the A.O.D.

16 FORWARD TRAILER SECTION

This unit was scaled to cover Canadian Corps and was used as planned. Its role was altered later by D.D.O.S. Canadian Army, who used it as an Army Troops Ordnance Field Park.

17 FORWARD TRAILER SECTION

Scaled to cover two Sherman Armoured Divisions and one Infantry Division. It was used as planned since its original scaling made it useful as an emergency holding for the Second British Army.

Certain of the Forward Trailer Sections, therefore, helped to ease the load of the Advanced Ordnance Depot which was able to supply them "in bulk" and thus by-pass from itself a substantial proportion of the detailed issues. Those Sections which really did operate forward were at the disposal of D.D.O.S., First and Second Army respectively, and available to him for such special tasks as arose during battle. The Sections in the L of C very soon overflowed on to the ground, so great was their stockholding, and they supplemented their over-worked military staff by large drafts of civilian labour.

While, therefore, not all the Forward Trailer Sections operated as planned—some did not go "forward"; others dispersed their "trailers"; others certainly outgrew the term "Section"—they each rendred invaluable aid during the campaign and helped to make the provision and supply of Ordnance stores so successful.

Ammunition Repair Units

Elsewhere records appear of the excellent work performed by the Ammunition Companies and the Base Ammunition Depots.

A number of Mobile Ammunition Repair Units also took part in the campaign, keeping well up with the line of advance so that they could scoop into forward depots the large quantities of British ammunition left behind from previous operations.

This ammunition they recovered and serviced so that it could be re-taken into stock "as new." One of these units—No. 1 Mobile Ammunition Repair Unit—was wholly employed in clearing, by demolition, stocks of unserviceable ammunition left behind in the advance.

The Field Ammunition Repair Factory at Antwerp received about 8,000 tons of doubtful ammunition and put back into service over 5,000 tons.

D.A.D.O.S. Dumps

The Ordnance representative in a Sub-Area is commonly known as the D.A.D.O.S. and is famous for his "Dump." This term hardly conveys a fair impression of the myriad small D.A.D.O.S. *depots* formed in the L of C. They had two prime functions. They received from the Advanced Ordnance Depot or from the Main Base, cases of stores for issue to units in their perimeter—issues made in response to indents which the units had demanded from them. These cases were opened, and the contents passed on to their respective units. To this extent, they were transit orgnaisations, making a retail issue on behalf of the wholesale depot—either an A.O.D. or, where the stores were not available in the theatre, a Central Ordnance Depot at home.

Their other function was to hold a stock of clothing and equipment (M.T. was covered by 14 Forward Trailer Section), in constant demand in order to make immediate issues of fast-moving items, and so eliminate the time-lag in obtaining these in small quantities from the

Base. In the L of C a D.A.D.O.S. Dump catered for upwards of 600 units—or the needs of anything up to 100,000 men. This might entail a turnover of 1,500 tons of stores per week.

RAOC Convoy Units

Much has already been said of the difficulty in obtaining transport for Ordnance stores, and of the special steps taken to form RAOC convoys to supply First and Second Armies in their rapid advance.

In the L of C a similar organisation sprung into being consisting of 24 3-ton lorries found from Ordnance resources. This unit brought up from the bridgehead to L of C Sub Area Dumps urgently needed stores, and like the Forward Area convoys, did fine work despite its *ad hoc* nature. Formed soon after the break-through in Normandy, it was retained as an essential element in the development of the long L of C which resulted from the chase of the retreating German Armies.

Officers' Shops

Officers' Shops were formed very early in the campaign to cater for the clothing and other requirements of all commissioned ranks in 21 Army Group. As early as July, one static shop was in being, and Mobile Officers' Shops soon followed the Armies on the basis of one to each Army and subsequently one shop was allocated to every Corps. Their arrival in an area was the only opportunity an Officer had of replenishing his hard worn kit, and their popularity and success were never in doubt. Personnel were found from disbanding Ordnance Beach Detachments, Port Ordnance Detachments etc., whose role was completed once the Normandy landing was made good.

The first static shop was opened in Bayeux, but as the campaign spread, others were established at Ghent, Brussels, Paris, Ostend, Herford, Hamburg, Iserlohn, Hannover, Neumunster, and Berlin.

The shop at Brussels, which was opened on the 2nd December 1944, achieved a turnover of £3,000 on its first day. After VE-day, sales settled down to an average of £4,500 a week.

When the first shop was opened, there was no standard form of accounting, and the skeleton military staff was faced with a problem that would stagger the boldest of commercial undertakings. Civilian shop assistants and cashiers had to be found and trained in large numbers. They had to be taught, in a language unfamiliar to them, the unusual Army terminology (drawers, woollen, long etc.). Worse still was the problem presented by the customers, who represented our cosmopolitian range of Allies. Business had to be conducted in as many as twelve languages !

The Officers' Shop organisation had, therefore, to grow at a terrific pace, finding new sites and fitting premises as well as maintaining its surprisingly large range of items. Over eleven hundred in number, they include all the clothing and equipment needs of both male and female officers.

A serious problem calling for drastic action was the alarming growth of the Black Market. Investigation showed that certain customers had purchased four or five pairs of shoes. It was discovered that a pair of shoes bought for a guinea in the Officers' Shop would fetch ten guineas in the black market. Although the offenders were few, the only solution was to introduce ration cards. This measure helped to cut down excess sales, and so conserve stocks to cover bona fide needs based on a fair ration for every officer.

It is imossible to compare the Ordnance Officers' Shops with even the largest civilian clothing and outfitting business. Altogether, the Shops in this theatre averaged £20,000 sales a week—sales made over the counter by multi-lingual saleswomen ! Undoubtedly, these shops brought a great deal of comfort into the lives of officers who had no other means of replacing their kit. Although only one sidelight of Ordnance, their importance and popularity were never in doubt.

Local Procurement

Local procurement played a notable part in providing Ordnance stores from resources found within the theatre. This department, working under the Senior Provision Officer (Local Resources) and also under a branch of the Ordnance Directorate, helped to ease the strain on shipping space by obtaining stores on the continent, and was also frequently called upon to produce items which would take too long to deliver from the Main Base.

S.P.O., Local Resources, found his staff originally from 17 Advanced Ordnance Depot, after the closing of that depot. The department was notified of Ordnance items in short supply and then endeavoured to locate a civilian firm capable of manufacturing them, if they were not already on sale. This invariably meant finding coal and raw materials in countries devastated by war—not an easy matter—and finally negotiating a contract at a price which would be approved by the Office of Mutual Aid.

By September, 1945, the Brussels branch alone had spent about £25,000,000 on stores produced in the theatre. More than 4,000 different kinds of stores had been supplied, many in enormous quantities : 500,000 packing cases, 550,000 pounds of paint, 465,000 shoulder titles, over 1,000,000 knives, forks and spoons, nearly 4,000,000 sacks, about 100,000 beds—these are afew of the items supplied. They ranged from "end connectors" for tanks, of which about 500,000 were produced, to anti-typhus sprays. The latter were locally manufactured to an American pattern, and must have helped to save countless lives.

The extended end connectors were a fitting to the tracks of Sherman tanks to give a firmer grip in soft ground. They widened the track by 25%, and gave a greater stability. As might be expected, the modification was required urgently, and very energetic action had at once to be taken by Ordnance to procure the modification stores. Another large-scale modification store which had to be produced in the theatre at short notice was a fitting to the headlamps of all "B" vehicles. This became necessary when, air attack having abated and the L of C suddenly lengthened, the speed of convoys had to be increased and stronger headlights were essential for safety. The cost of this modification was about £28,000, but production in the theatre enabled the change-over to be made more quickly, thereby saving precious days and hours.

Depot Control Companies

Finally, as the end of the war approached, the R.A.O.C. of 21 Army Group had to take over enemy stores dumps as well as German resources for the manufacture of warlike materials. The plan evolved was to create "teams," which could be sent swiftly to all parts of Germany. Several teams made up a Company and each Company was administered by a Chief Ordnance Officer. The scheme allowed great flexibility, and when the German Army collapsed, these teams took over numerous German Ordnance dumps and factories.

The heavy air bombardment to which the enemy had been subjected had produced a state of complete chaos throughout the Reich, and it was no easy task to create order in areas which had suffered from saturation bombing. Records were confused ; the local civilians, though willing enough to assist, seemed stunned by defeat, and the process of sorting serviceable equipment required much patience and skill. Items of use to the Allies were rescued and other war material unsuited to our needs was destroyed.

It is interesting to note that the quantity of serviceable stores found was not on anything like the scale that had been expected. There was no doubt that the enemy was on his knees when he capitulated, having used his reserves to the point of exhaustion.

CHAPTER X.

ORDNANCE FOR THE AIRBORNE LANDINGS

NIGHT after night, huge bomber fleets had roared their way over the south coast. But this night—or rather, early this morning—it was something different that was happening in the sky. Troops in the Embarkations Camps, others on their way to the "hards," still others on Landing Craft drawing in to the Normandy beaches—all these had been "briefed," and knew what was happening.

But back in the Concentration Areas along the southern coast of England were the "build-up" Formations, and they did not share the secret. Now, as hoards of airplanes flew low overhead, they stirred uneasily in their sleep. A few got up to peer into the sky. They saw swarms of planes, sure enough, *and the planes were towing gliders!* This was it! Camps soon came to life and buzzed with excitement as thousands of men awakened to see the most vivid and dramatic spectacle of their lives.

It was the great D-Eve offensive of the Sixth Airborne Division, The men of this gallant Division where the first to land on Normandy soil.

Few who saw them fly over the Channel on the dawn of D-day could have realised the amount of planning and co-ordination which preceeded this daring operation. In common with the other services, Ordnance had made its contribution. For an airborne operation differs from no other in the matter of maintenance—except that the provision of stores, ammunition and equipment is considerably harder.

Altogether, three mass airborne landings were undertaken by the British Liberation Army, and maintained by Ordnance. RAOC personnel took part in each and were able to render excellent service. Casualties, particularly in the Arnhem drop, were very heavy in proportion to the number of men engaged.

Planning the Normandy Drop

The Normandy landing of the Sixth Airborne Division was, however, the first time an Ordnance unit had actually dropped with the "Red Devils." Consequently, it created a record so far as time of entering into the theatre was concerned.

The planning of this particular operation centred around the answers to two questions facing the Ordnance HQ attached to the Sixth Airborne Division: they had to decide, first, what ways and means would be adopted of getting stores, ammunition and equipment into the theatre. Then they had to decide what part of the Ordnance organisation was required to take part in the actual flight.

This second problem was highly important. An airborne offensive has two phases, The opening phase is the only one which is really airborne. The flying troops are followed by a "seaborne tail," and obviously it is necessary to scale down the number of non-fighting men who take part in the first phase, so that it is given the maximum amount of "punch." Most of the Services follow-up in the seaborne tail.

For the Normandy drop, the Ordnance detachment was limited to platoon strength. Even so, the seaborne element was "due in" so soon afterwards that the last Ordnance personnel to enter the theatre in support of the Sixth Airborne Division arrived on D+2!

How Airborne Stores are Delivered

As to the other question which faced the Ordnance planning staff—how to get the stores and equipment into the hands of the airborne assault—four methods were considered and all, in fact, have been used at one time or another in North-west Europe :—

First, the Jettison Drop. Stores were packed in special containers which were then loaded into the bomb racks of planes and released automatically over the assembly area. The containers floated down by parachute.

Secondly, the Supply Drop. Stores planes flew over the assembly area. The containers were thrown out by hand, and parachuted down.

Thirdly, the Man-pack. The idea here was that each man should carry a special pack of stores on his person.

Fourthly, Glider Supply. Stores were packed into gliders which were towed to the assemby area, and then released.

The delivery and packing of stores for the Sixth Airborne Division were clearly matters of importance. On the efficiency of the methods adopted, the whole success of the operation turned. The scaling of these stores had also to receive the most earnest consideration. In view of the high wastage rates, it had to be liberal within the limits of the tonnage which the Air Force could drop.

The plan evolved was that the Ordnance Detachment to fly in with the assault wave should be prepared to maintain the Division for one to three weeks. By this time, it was foreseen, a link-up with the land force would be made, and the territory taken by airborne troops could be absorbed into the general beachhead.

Airborne Detachment in Action Three Months

As it happened, the handful of Ordnance personnel who were dropped—consisting of the A.D.O.S. of the Division and elements from the Divisional Ordnance Field Park—continued to function for three months, due to the stubborn resistance encountered in the beachhead.

Brigade Ordnance Warrant Officers dropped with their Brigades and they, with other members of the Ordnance Detachment, helped to collect the jettisoned containers and get the Ordnance dump going. The "supply drop" was also used to bring in reserves of stores, and containers fell within the collecting zone. It was found, however, that the parachutes attracted enemy fire and casualties were suffered in collecting the containers. At one stage, the battle became so furious that all the Ordnance personnel were snatched by the Parachute Battalions to take part in holding the vital Orne bridgehead, upon which depended the whole future of the operation.

The Divisional Maintenance Area was about the size of a football field, and in this area the Ordnance stores and ammunition dumps grew up cheek by jowl alongside petrol, food and other reserves. The ammunition was stacked around the fringe of the area, and Ordnance personnel—when not engaged in fighting—lived, moved, slept and had their being among the stacks from which they issued.

In the small hours of one morning, a concentrated barrage was put down on the dump and much of the ammunition exploded. Decorations were won by members of the Ordnance Detachment for putting out, with their bare hands, fires which smouldered among the ammunition.

Eventually when the hard core of enemy resistance began to crumble, the Sixth Airborne Division was withdrawn to re-equip and prepare for a future operation. This proved to be the crossing of the Rhine.

The Arnhem Drop

Meanwhile, the Arnhem drop was mounted by the gallant troops of the First Airborne Division, whose eight day battle came so near to victory.

This operation was unique, in that no airborne landing before or since has seen Ordnance paratroops and glider-borne troops play so full a part. Altogether, the party numbered 28

Officers and men. When the order came for the Arnhem force to retire, one only was the reported strength of the RAOC at the reception centre. We shall see what happened to the others.

The Arnhem battle raged for eight days. It was fought to the limit of human endurance. Hunger, thirst and a dearth of supplies cast a shadow over the operations which daily grew longer. Nor, as things worked out, was anyone in a position to exert an influence over these factors. From an Ordnance point of view, the enterprise was a disappointment in that the stores did not get through. It had been planned to fly in maintenance stores and equipment over a period of several days, but only a fraction of the items scaled ever came into possession of the airborne Ordnance Field Park.

To appreciate the situation it is necessary to recapitulate the tactical developments which gave rise to the Arnhem expedition. After their headlong retreat from Falaise, the Germans had contrived to form a continous line on the Escaut-Meuse canal. The Allied object was to smash this line, leap the rivers Maas and Rhine in one great bound, and so place themselves in a position to draw into the North German plain.

Three airborne forces were accordingly earmarked and equipped for the battle. They were the 1st Airborne Division, a British formation, which was to land at Arnhem, and thereby achieve the most forward thrust into the enemy's side; and the American 82nd and 101st Airborne Divisions, which were chosen to land at Nijmegen and Eindhoven.

Second Army were to push, coincident with these landings, to effect a landward link-up and turn the flank of the West wall.

Arnhem, besides being the objective, was undoubtedly the key-piece in the battle, since it had road and rail bridges over the river Rhine.

D-Day for the Arnhem Drop

D-day was the 17th of September. On that fateful Sunday morning, more than 3,000 aircraft rose up from 25 British 'dromes and sped towards their Holland rendezvous. The force included Stirlings, Halifaxes, Dakotas, fighter planes of various types, and a great armada of tug-planes towing gliders packed with men and equipment.

It was a bold, brave enterprise and, with average luck, it might well have proved a successful one. The landing sites were well behind the German defence line. No heavy concentrations of fighting troops were expected, least of all two Panzer Divisions which, by one of those strange and unpredictable hazards of war, had just been withdrawn to Arnhem for re-equipment. This, then, was the dice we had not gambled on, but it was to turn up, unexpectedly, to throw the whole game against us at the most critical moment, pinning our men down till the surprised and baffled enemy had mustered up re-inforcements. It was the unforeseen factor which was to foil, far more by accident than enemy design, the main object of our plan.

This ominous concentration of enemy armour was happily concealed to the men who flew over the English coast on the 17th and 18th of September. On D-day, the Ordnance paratroops had descended with the spearhead. The detachment consisted of one officer and five men. Their task: to recce. the ground and prepare for the arrival of the Ordnance Field Park and Ordnance HQ. But fate decreed that they should never see their colleagues again—until several months later, when the war was over and won! Four of the party were wounded, and the whole lot taken prisoners, when the tide of the battle surged against us.

The Main Party, who followed by glider, consisted of the A.D.O.S. and eight men, and the airborne Ordnance Field Park, staffed by one officer and ten O.R.'s. They took off on the morning of the 18th of September, and landed with the bulk of the Division.

One Plane Beleagured

On the flight over, one of the Ordnance gliders had its tow-rope severed by an A.A. shell, and had to make a forced landing "somewhere in Holland." It was a bitter disappointment to the men aboard to know, as their plane glided down into enemy territory far from the rendezvous, that their part in the Arnhem offensive was over even before it had begun. They made a good landfall, and set off to find a hiding place. They were helped by the Dutch underground and had some exciting experiences. These also had an amusing aspect, the joke being appreciated better in retrospect! The party finally took refuge on the top of a tall, covered haystack, against which someone had providentially left a ladder.

Every night one of the party descended this ladder to gather fruit and other edibles. All went well till one night the "shopper" returned to find the ladder lying on the ground. It had been knocked down, presumably, by a horse in the field. But supposing someone had passed in the interval and noticed that the ladder lay on the ground—to set it up again would arouse suspicion. The "shopper" decided that the best thing to do was to leave the ladder where it lay and mount the haystack on the back of the obliging horse. This was all very well in theory, but he was not to foresee that the horse would take fright when he was decently mounted, and bolt off in the direction of the village, where the enemy were billited! By good luck, the beast pulled up short of the houses, was persuaded to retrace its steps, and the luckless soldier was at length deposited safely back in his hiding place, none the worse for his experience.

This party was to have one more humorous adventure. When news came to the village that the Germans were pulling out, secret preparations were made to fete the British soldiers who had sought asylum there. In due course, the party was carried off in triumph to the village hall. Judge, then, the mortification of some hardened Canadian infanteers who, knowing nothing of this, stole up to the village hall at the height of the celebrations, expecting to find the Germans still in occupation! Instead they were confronted by the spectacle of an Ordnance sub-conductor making a victory speech to Dutch villagers who had assembled to toast their liberation!

So much for the glider which broke free. What of the Recce party who had parachuted into the blue on D-day? Here, in diary form, is a record of their experiences: it leaves no doubt as to the wisdom of their training, which had been designed to make them soldiers in the fullest sense of the term:

Recce Party's Log-Book

Sunday, 17 September: 1045–1130. Fitting parachutes and equipment preparatory to making flight. Men in good spirits.

1148 *hrs.* Take off.

1403 *hrs.* Landed in Holland. Weather ideal for "jump" and the "stick" was well concentrated. Everyone R.V'd as instructed. Flak light, but some ground opposition on outskirts of Dropping Zone.

1500 *hrs.* 1 Brigade HQ started moving into Arnhem. A fair amount of sniping, which was effectively dealt with by LMG's.

2000 *hrs.* We had gained control of the Northern end of the road bridge. We were about company strength. The Ordnance O.C. took over a house on close perimeter defence of the bridge and his detachment was strengthened by six O.R.'s of R. Signals. There was confused fighting all night, with heavy enemy mortar and M.G. fire. It was dangerous to move about outside because of the light from burning buildings.

Monday, 18 *September.* Some German armoured cars crossed the bridge from the South bank. A/tank gunners stopped the vehicles while we knocked out the crews as they tried to get away. Enemy mortar fire very heavy, and buildings were being destroyed all around. We had some casualties. Later, twin Oerlikons opened up on us from the bridge.

Tuesday, 19 *September.* Plenty of German armour about this morning. It seemed fairly certain that the armour had broken through our outer defences and that we were cut off. Our men in good shape and taking advantage of any target offered. Spotted five Jerries trying to connect-up the charges to blow the bridge and kept them under observation till able to knock the lot out in one burst. About 1800 hrs., some elements of 1 Bn. succeeded in getting through to us but were later driven back again. The night was almost as bright as the day from the flames of burning buildings. One of our defended houses went up. Patrol found that our crew had evacuated to another house—they had been grenaded out, with severe casualties. Other houses occupied later had to be evacuated. Under darkness, made our way to river bank and barricaded ourselves under one of the spans of the bridge.

Wednesday, 20 September. Soon after daybreak, the fireworks started. We had found some Oerlikon ammunition stored in one of the pillars of the bridge, while on the bridge itself were mounted two twin Oerlikons. We proposed to capture the Oerlikons and started barricading the steps up the bridge to make some sort of cover. The Germans turned heavy 88 mm. fire on us and drove us off the steps. They also started blasting a hole through the pillar where the ammunition was stored with the object of blowing it up. The Western side of our archway was screened by a building, but Jerry quickly reduced this to rubble and we came under fire on both sides from Mark VI's, mortar and LMG's. Decided to withdraw to the next archway. This was done without loss but the position did not improve because Tiger tanks were closing in. We were powerless to stop them because we were out of Piat bombs. Finally decided to get back to the main force outside of the town.   (Here the extract ends abruptly.)

The rest of the story is of withdrawal. The Ordnance detachment was caught in the net, however, and with their capitualtion ended all resistance on the bridge. They had not been dropped to fight, but to receive and issue stores. There were no stores, however, so they fought bravely on, holding the vital bridge till entirely surrounded and overcome.

Adventures of the Main Glider Party

Meanwhile, the Main Party was having a somewhat similar experience. On landing, they were not met at the rendezvous, since the recce. party were cut off. So they decided to join up with Divisional HQ and sited the Field Park and Ordnance HQ in this area.

In England arrangements had been made for automatic supplies to be dropped to cover the anticipated requirements of the force. But the dropping site was never captured, and only a fraction of the stores landed in the narrowing bridgehead. The rest floated down either on sites still in enemy hands, or in No Man's Land, from whence they could not be retrieved.

As each day passed, the situation worsened. The precious strip of liberated Holland gradually diminished in size. Meanwhile, further attempted drops of badly needed stores continued, with little advantage. Jeeps, trailers, gun parts, wireless spares—all these had been scaled, but few got through to the Field Park. Wireless parts were particularly in demand to replace damage caused to sets in landing.

During all this time the Ammunition Examiner was one of the busiest members of the Ordnance party. Ammunition dropped from the air often requires inspection to avoid prematures, and the services of the Examiner were also needed to deal with unexploded bombs and shells which the Germans had dropped inside the perimeter, and also to inspect captured enemy ammunition. Other members of the Ordnance detachment took part in patrols, all had their defence tasks.

From Bad to Worse

As the week drew slowly to its close, the situation deteriorated further. We had suffered heavy casualties. Our small force was outnumbered, and outweighted in firepower. Morale remained high, but this and courage alone were not enough to turn the tide of battle. We were burnt out of one defensive position after another.

"The British fought like lions," said one enemy commentator. "They made themselves strong in houses and gardens. Every window became a fire-spitting fortress, every basement a machine-gun nest. Only when the roof caved in, the tall walls crumbled, and the whole house was about to be devoured by a sheet of flame, did they leave these strongholds. They were the most hardy warriors we have met in the whole invasion. They resisted to the end with knives and pistols."

But now it really was the end. The long-awaited breakthrough of Second Army had not come. At length the order came to evacuate across the river under cover of darkness. The Ordnance party formed up at 10 p.m. On their way down to the river bank, they ran into a German machine-gun position, suffering heavy casualties, including three killed. One man alone got through.

What Arnhem Achieved

But Arnhem was not a failure. We did not succeed in exploiting it in the manner planned. The airborne troops clung to the ground by their teeth till the situation was quite hopeless. Second Army did not come. But they did surge forward sixty miles to Nijmegen, and it was from this base later that fresh operations commenced which were to send the enemy reeling to disaster.

The officers and men of the RAOC who served, and fought, in this brave operation, are listed below :—

Ordnance HQ

(i) *Advance Parachute Recce Party*

Capt. B. V. Manley	P.O.W.	
S/Sgt. Walker	P.O.W.	Wounded
Pte. Mordecai.	P.O.W.	Wounded
Pugh	P O W	Wounded
McCarthy	P.O.W.	Wounded
Heany	P.O.W.	

(ii) *Main Glider Party*

Lt.Col. G.A. Mobbs	P.O.W.	Wounded
S/Cdr. G. E. Jenkins		
S/Cdr. Eastwood		
S/Sgt. Brown	Missing	
Sgt. Bennet	Wounded	
Cpl. Coppenhall	P.O.W.	
Pte. Hodges	P.O.W.	
Gibson	Wounded	Missing
Browning	P.O.W.	

Ordnance Field Park

Major G. C. Chidgey	P.O.W.	Wounded
S/Sgt. Wilson	P.O.W.	Wounded
Sgt. Plowman		
Sgt. Andrews		Missing
Cpl. Thompson	P.O.W.	
Cpl. Congley		
Pte. Horsley	P.O.W.	
Pooley	P.O.W.	Wounded
Wright	P.O.W.	Wounded
Wynn	P.O.W.	Wounded
Cpl. Grantham	Killed	
S/Cdr. Higham	P.O.W.	Wounded
S/Cdr. Halsall	P.O.W.	Wounded

The Rhine Drop

Bearing in mind the lessons of the two preceding airborne operations, when Ordnance men were used in an infantry role, only a few "key" personnel were dropped on the Rhine crossing. They came in by glider. Gliders were also the chief means adopted for the delivery of stores.

The Sixth Airborne Divisional Field Park was held on the West bank of the Rhine, to enter the theatre by land at the appointed time.

On this occasion the airborne troops were being used in a new way: not, as previously, to land unexpectedly and prepare the way for a later landward offensive. They were dropped *after* the land offensive had been begun, to exploit and develop the confusion and chaos which the infantry and armoured spearheads would achieve among the enemy in the bridge-head.

The Sixth Airborne Divisional Field Park lost no time in establishing a forward holding on the Eastern bank of the Rhine, and airborne troops eventually reachead the Baltic where they joined our Russian allies at Wismar on 2nd May. Their maintenance during this period of exploitation was no simple matter. The Ordnance Field Parks of all Formations had a great variety of "customers" calling hastily for stores and equipment, battle casualties were replaced, and the assault swept exuberantly on.

In no theatre before has Ordnance played so large a role in airborne operations. The courage of those who took part sometimes amounted to heroism, as in the gallant Arnhem offensive. RAOC officers and men attached to the First and Sixth Airborne Divisions can be no prouder of their red berets than their Corps is proud of them. They helped to make history and, in the making of it, hurried the war all the quicker to its triumphant end.

CHAPTER XI

CANADA'S STIRRING CONTRIBUTION

SO far, in this history, attention has been focussed on the part played by the British Ordnance units under command of 21 Army Group. This arrangement was decided for convenience in telling the story of the campaign.

But now the time has come to pay tribute to the brilliant work of the Canadians. As fighting troops, the world knows them second to none. Their Ordnance services throughout the battle in North-West Europe were equal to every demand which their Army imposed : no better compliment could be made than that ! The Royal Canadian Ordnance Corps has a reputation of which, but for the spirit that animates the Service generally, their British cousins might well feel envious.

Once again, our narrative reaches back to the strenuous planning period which led up to D-day. Side by side with the Ordnance Directorates at 21 Army Group and at the Second British Army, the Canadian Ordnance HQ at First Army were making preparations for the maintenance of a very considerable force.

Events Before D-day

But even this is not the beginning of the tale. Once before, on the Continent of Europe, the Canadians had planned and staged their own private D-day.

The name "Dieppe" glistens in Allied military annals, recalling a stirring action fought against overwhelming odds. It brought us priceless information about the enemy's coastal defences, his counter-invasion tactics, his weapons.

At one time it had been hoped that when the First Canadian Army took part in the invasion it would have both 1 and 2 Canadian Corps under command. However, global warfare had made heavy inroads on the Canadian Army's assets. The Second Canadian Corps were available in England, but the First Canadian Corps were thousands of miles away, fighting with the Eighth Army, and could not be spared. The whole force did not, in fact, meet together in the theatre until February 1945, by which time France, Belgium and most of Holland were liberated, and everything was poised for the last great "swan" into Germany.

The First Canadians In

The plan adopted was that 3 Canadian Infantry Division and 2 Canadian Armoured Brigade were detached from the First Army and absorbed into 1 Corps of the British Second Army. They were given the central (Juno) sector to attack—see plan on page 18. Furthermore, the Canadian Parachute Battalion landed as part of the Sixth Airborne Division, and engaged in the valiant defence of the Eastern flank of the original beachhead.

The first Canadian Ordnance units to land were :—

3 Infantry Division Ordnance Field Park,

2 Armoured Brigade Ordnance Field Park,

7 Canadian Mobile Landing and Bath Unit,

and a detachment of the Canadian Ordnance Maintenance Company.

—all these units did a grand job throughout the campaign.

The remainder of the Ordnance units came in with the First Canadian Army, which had been held in reserve during the actual assault and was not due in pursuant to the pre-invasion plan, until Caen had fallen, but in view of the enemy's invasion stand, landed in mid-July. Soon those Canadian formations which were already ashore had a grim foretaste of what was to prove the First Army's role so often in this campaign. Time and again, the Canadians were assigned the hard, grinding task of pounding an enemy strong position until, by sheer force and persistence, it was reduced to ashes. For example, Caen was the hinge of the enemy's whole defensive system. If Caen broke, everything broke. The Canadian units which kept hammering away at this super fortress were alive to the great possibilities before them. Ultimately, however, the bulk of the First Canadian Army disembarked before Caen had been captured. When at length the Allies smashed their way yard by yard into the town, the 3rd Canadian Division was in the forefront of the battle.

Planning the Falaise Route

Ordnance was under stern test during all these critical battles. "Wastage" rates were high, in view of the intensive nature of the fighting; but the RCOC rose to the occasion, and the Canadian troops were "fed" by a continuous stream of supplies.

Towards the end of July, the First Canadian Army was fighting as an Army. Its main task was to form the left pincer of the great Allied operations designed to capture Falaise, and the destruction in the famous "pocket" of the Seventh German Army.

Two attacks had to be put in before Falaise fell. The first over-ran the enemy's defences, but he managed to reform on another strong line just north of Falaise. The second offensive was launched on the 14th of August, and the result was the capture of Falaise and the closing of the pocket on the 19th when formations of the Canadian Army met the Americans at Chambas. Overnight, static warfare vanished from the scene: the way was opened out for a mobile offensive on a staggering scale! The Canadians who fought so bravely in the early days around Caen could hardly have imagined what now lay before them. Inside a month of the break-through at Caen, the Allies were writing their names across the map of Europe. Canadian Ordnance units followed the First Army up to the Seine, and then on to Rouen, Le Havre, St. Omer and Ypres.

Then, on the 1st of September, history in reverse, but how differently it was to be enacted! This time, it was the Germans who retired from Dieppe and without putting up a fight at all! In August, 1942, the Second Canadian Infantry Division had made their historic landing at Dieppe: it was the same formation which entered Dieppe now, ready to avange their first penetration—but only a madly cheering army of French civilians remained to receive them!

The First Army had been given the command to clear the coastal belt, and the coastal belt was one of Hitler's strong cards: it simply swarmed with fortresses. Not all the coast towns fell so easily as Dieppe—all the way up, it was a stiff but victorious struggle.

The Transport Problem

During the long push up from Normandy, the major worry of the Ordnance staff of First Army was not the provision of Ordnance stores and ammunition. Their scaling was good, and they did not have many worries on that score. The crowning anxiety was transport, and transport they could not get. At times, the situation seemed desperate and eventually they were left with no alternative but to "ground" the Field Parks and other wheeled units, and send their vehicles back to the Normandy base to bring forward the needed replacements.

In the pre-D-day planning, Brigadier Bennett, Deputy Director of Ordnance Services, First Army, had decided, from his experience in Italy, that formations should land with the largest possible reserve of stores in their own transport. This helped to maintain the force in the first heavy battles around Caen, when immense expenditure took place. D.D.O.S., First Army had also re-scaled the Canadian Ordnance Field Parks, stepping-up the holdings about 50 per cent. Extra vehicles and trailers were provided to carry these increased holdings. For example, authority was obtained to furnish each of the Canadian Ordnance Sub-Parks with 20 ten-tonners instead of three-tonners. Two tank transporters were obtained for the Corps Field Parks, and when the sides of these transporters were built up, they were able to carry a volume of about 75 tons of stores!

These two factors—the increased scaling and the additional vehicles—were always to exercise an important influence over the supply problems of First Army. The stores were available *in bulk*, and when the RASC transport was allocated on priority tasks of carrying petrol and ammunition, Ordnance Field Parks dropped their holdings on the ground and used their transport for *ad hoc* convoys from the Rear Maintenance Area.

All through the campaign, fairly heavy reserves of stores were often left behind in the L of C. At the beginning of the big push, 2 Corps reserve of Vote 7 and 8 stores amounted to about 4,000 tons. This was "eaten down" in the battle from Caen to Ghent. In the Corps supply lane, the D.D.O.S. ultimately had as many as nine dumps spread out all along the L of C! Ordnance transport was constantly on the move, travelling to and from the Rear Maintenance Area, and if this transport had not been available, it is doubtful if the force could have been maintained.

The run-up from Normandy was made more difficult by the number of bridges which had been blown. At the Seine bridge, the tank transporters were emptied of their stores, made an empty trip over the Seine "Bailey," and then had to be re-loaded on the far bank by ferrying the stores across the bridge piecemeal in three-tonners!

The Fight to free Antwerp

By the end of September, the First Canadian Army had advanced from Caen to Holland—a distance of 300 miles—without the assistance of an important sea-port. Arnhem had been a glorious failure, the long and magnificent era of mobile warfare had ended, and it became now more than ever urgent, not only for the benefit of the First Army but for 21 Army Group as a whole, that the key port of Antwerp should be quickly converted to our use. Antwerp port we held securely, but access from the sea was still denied us by the enemy, who was strongly entrenched in the Scheldt mouth. He knew that once Antwerp was in use, it would become the perfect base for our invasion of Germany proper. He therefore decided to contest its use to the bitter end, and once again the First Army was given a hard nut to crack. The result was two peculiar but analagous operations conducted by 2 Canadian Corps: first, to clear the south bank of the Scheldt (which was done by 3 Canadian Division); second, to clear Walcheren and South Beveland.

The Scheldt operation was done by the Third Canadian Infantry Division—the same which had been singled out for the original D-day operations. Fighting was as bitter and as merciless as on the initial landing. The "ground" was water; conditions could hardly have been worse. Nevertheless, the Hun resisted with fanatical courage, knowing how much depended on the outcome.

The Walcheren Expedition

Such fighting is hard on men, but it is equally hard on equipment. The Ordnance contribution was all-important to success. Much special equipment was specially flown over from England for this and the second analagous operation—the clearance of Walcheren and South Beveland. This latter task was done by the Second Canadian Infantry Division, by the Fourth Commando Brigade and, towards the end, by the 52nd British Lowland Division. It was really an amphibious operation.

How easily the best laid plans can miscarry is illustrated by a situation which arose in mounting the Walcheren assault. Water for drinking purposes simply did not exist on the ground to be captured, and no water trucks could go with the assault troops. So the Deputy Director of Ordnance Services, First Army, arranged for a special train of water "jerricans" to be brought forward from the Rear Maintenance Area. As the time drew on for the assault, this train had not arrived. Then it was found that "Q" staff had stopped the train midway on the journey, the jerricans had been dumped, and the train sent back to bring up ammunition! Immediately there began a frantic round-up of all the milk-cans in Holland: these were collected by the Salvage branch of the Royal Canadian Ordnance Corps, swapped for the jerricans of Army Troops, and the jerricans rushed in the nick of time to the assault troops, who were now all ready to make the Walcheren attack.

With both the Scheldt Estuary and South Beveland-Walcheren positions reduced, the First Army presented the glittering prize of Antwerp to the theatre. Thus, the new "advanced base" rapidly came into being, and thereafter problems of transport and supply were never on the same scale for any of the Services.

On to the Siegfried Line

The First Army then took over the Nijmegen bridgehead and, after the failure of von Rundstedt's Ardennes counter-attack, began the task of clearing the area between the rivers Meuse and Rhine. Memories of Caen must have haunted Canadian minds in those days, for this sector contained the northern "hinge" of the Siegfried Line. Once again the First Army had been assigned the task of smashing a focal point! Very heavy casualties in men and equipment were suffered. Elements of ten enemy divisions joined issue, but eventually the German was driven back. This, and the clearance of the enemy from Eastern and Western Holland, paved the way for the final assault towards Emden and Wilhelmshaven. Ultimately, with the German capitulation, over 180,000 of the enemy surrendered to the First Army.

Canadian Ordnance Organisation

The Canadian Ordnance organisation is slightly different from the British. For example, salvage comes under Ordnance. RCOC personnel are not encouraged to specialise to quite the same extent as British Ordnance: a Laundry Officer may be drafted to a Field Park, and *vice versa*. Every Canadian Division has its "Ordnance area" where the Field Park, Salvage, Laundry etc., facilities are located together, usually all under command of the Senior Ordnance Officer.

Ordnance supply problems in the campaign arose mainly in connection with transport, and we have seen how the RCOC devised its own salvation here. In addition to the Field Park and other transport which was whipped in to form Ordnance convoys, replacement vehicles coming up to First Army from Vehicle Parks in the Rear Maintenance Area were loaded with stores for which the forward echelons were waiting.

Always the supply of Vote 9 Stores—M.T., armament, signal, wireless etc.—was good, but around Christmas a crisis arose in the supply of clothing. For two months or so the position remained grave, and the lack of transport, due to the extended L of C, only served to aggravate this problem.

However, the provision and supply of warlike stores was consistently excellent. The case of the Second Canadian Division is an example. This division was thrown into the Caen battle and for weeks pushed doggedly on, gaining and yielding ground inch by inch, facing tremendous opposition. The strain began to tell but the Canadians kept hammering away, pulling the enemy to the left flank while the Americans swung round the side. As a result of this persistent battering, the Division sustained heavy casualties in men and equipment. But the Ordnance service was so good that the bulk of Vote 9 replacements were effected within 24 hours, some within 12 hours and the rest within 36!

The Units Which Took Part

The Canadian Ordnance units which took part in the campaign were as follows:—

1 Canadian Infantry Divisional Ordnance Field Park.
2 Canadian Infantry Divisonal Ordnance Field Park.
3 Canadian Infantry Divisional Ordnance Field Park.
4 Canadian Armoured Divisional Ordnance Field Park.
5 Canadian Armoured Divisional Ordnance Field Park.
1 Canadian Armoured Brigade Ordnance Field Park.
2 Canadian Armoured Brigade Ordnance Field Park.
201 Canadian Infantry Ordnance Sub-Park.
202 Canadian Infantry Ordnance Sub-Park.
203 Canadian Infantry Ordnance Sub-Park.

204 Canadian Armoured Ordnance Sub-Park.
205 Canadian Armoured Ordnance Sub-Park.
1 Canadian Corps Army Troops Ordnance Sub-Park.
2 Canadian Corps Army Troops Ordnance Sub-Park.
3 Canadian Corps Army Troops Ordnance Sub-Park.
1 Canadian Salvage Collecting Centre.
2 Canadian Salvage Collecting Centre.
3 Canadian Salvage Collecting Centre.
4 Canadian Salvage Collecting Centre.
5 Canadian Salvage Collecting Centre.
1 Canadian Salvage Unit.
2 Canadian Salvage Unit.
3 Canadian Salvage Unit.
1 Canadian Mobile Laundry and Bath Unit.
2 Canadian Mobile Laundry and Bath Unit.
3 Canadian Mobile Laundry and Bath Unit.
4 Canadian Mobile Laundry and Bath Unit.
5 Canadian Mobile Laundry and Bath Unit.
6 Canadian Mobile Laundry and Bath Unit.
7 Canadian Mobile Laundry and Bath Unit.
8 Canadian Mobile Laundry and Bath Unit.
9 Canadian Mobile Laundry and Bath Unit.
1 Corps Troops Ordnance Field Park.
2 Corps Troops Ordnance Field Park.
Canadian Ordnance Maintenance Company.
Detachments of the Canadian Central Ordnance Depot.
16 Forward Trailer Section (a British unit under command D.D.O.S., First Army).
144 (British) Vehicle Park.

A Splendid Achievement

Right through the planning period, and from D-day onward, the co-operation which 21 Army Group received from Ordnance units and representatives of First Army was outstanding. A smaller Ordnance organisation than the Second Army, in virtue of the reduced size of the force, it was nevertheless substantial and always carried a heavy load.

All who have served with the Canadians will never forget their zeal and efficiency, the spirit in which they set about performing sometimes impossible tasks, and the "drive" for which their nation is famous. The First Army's battles were tough, courageous and usually, as it happened, fought in very bad country. That these same battles succeeded so brilliantly, was due in part to the magnificent service of the Royal Canadian Ordnance Corps. They saw that the stores and equipment were always at hand, all along the coast and hinterland from Normandy to Walcheren—and beyond!

CHAPTER XII

RAOC HONOURS AND AWARDS

C.B.E.

Brig.	J.G. Denniston
	W. Palmer
	T.H. Clarke
Col.	F.H. Mackenzie
	A.N.C. Varley

O.B.E.

Brig.	L.E. Cutforth
	J.C. Waycott
,,	R.C. Hiam
Col.	L.H. Worskett
	B. McEwan
	B.A.P. Lambert
	W.T. Grimsdale
	P.R. Hill
	W.A. Kenney
	L.A. Mahoney
	R. Volkers
,,	A. Huddleston
Lt.Col.	R.C. Gibb
	G.W. Hayley
	T. Boyes
	R.G. Hicks
	E.N. Highton
	G.R. Kerr
	H.O. Robinson
	E.J. Smith
	F.R.H. Villiers
	A.H. White
	W. Perfect
,,	H.E. Simpster
	P.B. Thomson
,,	W.F. Tuson
Col.	G.N. Warnock
Lt.Col.	G. Wray
	L.E. Baker
	R.V. Blundell
	D.D. Dennis
,,	G.A.L. Freer
Col.	T.G. Gore
Lt. Col.	E.A. Horsey
Capt.	C.D. Kay
Lt.Col.	V.A. Lines
	G. Macdonald
	W. Martin
Capt.	H.L. Smith
Lt. Col.	F.W.S. Walker
	N. Carroll
	G. Chappell
	E.B. Stewart-Smith
	P.R. Sandars
	J. Hall
	E.V. Ranson
	F.E. Manning
	W.A. Hildred
	M. Barnes
	W. Elliott
	J.P.R. Howland

M.B.E.-Officers

Lt.Col.	F.T. Kellett
	R.H. Brown
	J.R. Roberts
	R.H. Goodfellow
	G.A. Goodman
	A.S. Ellick
	R.P. Morton
	G.D. Petts
Major	D.R. Bateman
	H. Brakes
	J. Snowball
	G. Stidwell
	N.E. Britton
	L.A.B. Cooke
	W.L. Holloway
	G.E. Hubbard
	R. Marshall
	A.L. Martin
	I.M. Mills
	C.H. Platten
	R.L. Streather
	F.G Rudham
	B.W. Grist
	G.A. Marfell
	R.J. Saunders
	J.E. Tucker (R.C.O.C.)
	E.W. Williams
	W.G. Henham
	W.M.L. Howard
	R.H. Bromley

Major	S. Seymour Baker
"	G.D. Berry
"	R.A. Hume
"	D.F. Farley
"	R.O. Milnes
"	R.L. Kenyon
"	W.J. Newton
"	H.J. Masters
"	A.H. Parnaby
"	W. Parker
"	W.F. d'A Spencer
"	D.A. Ronsham
"	H.M. Vickerman
"	J.S. Thompson
Capt.	W. Cavanagh
"	E. Lane
"	W.R.B. Burnett
"	E. Richardson
"	R.F. Davidson
"	A.G. Keest
"	A.D. Milroy
"	J. O'Connell
"	C.D. Costello
"	A.D. Cheers
"	J.C. Daglish
"	A. Kerr
"	R.H. Latham
"	G.B. Lucas
"	R. McEwen
"	R.J. Meech
"	H.L. Smith
"	J.B. Fisher
"	J.W. Gardiner
Lieut.	E. Atkins
"	P.T. Handford
"	G.D. Lucas

M.C.

| Capt. | F.N. Lowe |

George Medal

| Lt. Col. | G.C.G. Pepper |

M.B.E.—WOs and NCOs

W.O.I	J. Caldwell
	P.T. Harcup
	A. Booth
	L.J. Hasel
	W.J.H. Jones
	A. Kerr
	G.D. Lucas
	W. Rudd
	H.W. Griffiths
	McAlister
	E.F. O'Brien

W.O.I	W. Price
	L.S. Turner
	G.L. Bray
	W. Mitchell
	B.J.A. Pearce
	N. Oxley
	W.J. Rees
	G. Rushforth
	G.E. Woods
	W. Whitehead
"	I.G. Wilmshurst
W.O.II	K. Bentham
	C.J. Jewhurst

B.E.M.

S/Sjt.	F. Cahill
"	R. West
"	G. Hurst
Sjt.	J. Cross
Cpl.	J.E. Shaw

M.I.D.—Officers

Brig.	L.E. Cutforth, O.B.E.
"	J.G. Denniston, C.B.E.
Col.	B. Burkin
"	H.H. Fitton
Lt.Col.	N.E.R. Carroll
	D.D. Dennis
	W.A. Hildred
	J.R. Howarth
	R.W. Amoore
	A.S. Barker, M.C.
	F.N. Parker
	G.C. Pritchett
	E.B. Stewart-Smith
	R.D.R. Bateman
	K.A. Lines
	L. Mern
	F.W.S. Walker, O.B.E.
	J.T.C. Wykes
	G. Wray
Maj.	R.F. Davidson
	B.J.H. Griffiths
	H.S. Harris
	F.E. Manning
	R.J. Meech
	R.P. Morton
	G. Roberts
	C.N. Rolston
	W.L. Walder
	D.H. Williams
	J.T. Briggs
	W.F. Caldwell
	D.W. Crapper
	A.S. Ellick
	C.H. Hooper

Maj.	A.L. Marti	Capt.	B. Clements
	A.H. Parnaby		J. McK. Ferrier
	E.A. Pinson		G.W.A. Fielder
	S. Wooldridge		W.J. Hardesty
	G.D. Berry		W.J.S. Harper
	H.A. Ballatine		R.B. Kaufmann
	G.B. Bancroft		C.F. Kinnear
	M.F. Barnard		W. Kirkby
	W.W.H. Butler		G. Lawson M.C.
	L.C. Cunnell		R.N. Mellor
	J.E. Duckham		P.E.C. Durrant-Oxley
	B.J.H. Griffiths		S.F. Peace
	D.W. Heath		H.J. Perham
	A.H. Humble		W.L. Persson
	F.A. Jones		F.G. Pittam
	M.W. Lambert		D.H. Punter
	S.G. Lee		C. Rafferty
	H.J. Masters		W.H. Struthers
	H.T. May		F.J. Tavenor
	J.H.G. Pearce		H.H. Towle
	J.G. Perrin		K.S. Wilkinson
	G.D. Petts		R.F. Anness
	J.B. Pritchard		N. Archer
	D.T. Rowlatt		J.W. Barrett
	P.W. Russell		L.E. Berry
	E.L. Siebert		J. Brotherston
	W.F. d'A Spencer		A.V. Cant
	T.L. Sutton		K.J. Cluett
	W.L. Taylor		G.E. Daniels
	J.C. Timmins		H.E. Davis
	G.P. Whillier		J.F. Escott
	D.R. Widdowson		R.G.M. Hamm
	T.C. Williams		J.C. Hogg
	A.M.J.A.G. de Borman		W. Hughes
	H. Brook		R.R. MacEwan
	H.F. Compton		E.G.W. Malindine
	H.W.J.L. Cummins		J.E. Marks
	W. Elgin		J.A. McGill
	R.A. Handover		J.L. McKinlay
,,	H.M. Vickerman		G.F. Morris
Capt.	G.R. Rawes		G. Olding
	F.W. Appleby		J. Perry
	W.H. Chapman		F.G. Pittam
	D.F. Dykes		C.A. Richards
	C.C. Foster		W.S. Thomson
	J.F. Gallichan		E.B.E. Tucker
	H.I. Huggins		F.N. Tuckey
	A.G. Llewellyn		J. Whitwam
	J.R. Lucey		L.B. Wilson
	A.D. Milroy		A. Woods
	E.J. Palmer	,,	K.D. Zerny
	R.W. Pettit	Lieut.	A.F. Swarbrick
	G. Quarenden		A. Blooman
	R.J. Shaw		S.B. Gill
	G.F.R. Smith		A. Kerr
	W.S. Taylor		W. Stirk
	D.K. Wiltshire		J.A. Amess
	J.R. Brown		T.W. Baxter

Lieut.	E.L. Bristoll	W.O.II.	H.H.G. Cox
	A.E. Casban		L.H. Dodd
	J.F. Craven		N.F. Garrod
	S.D Eames		H.W. Grant
	L. Hopkinson		G. Jamieson
	J.H. Ness		J.N. Knott
	J.P. Dinder		V. Maguire
	F. Rangeley		W.H. McArtney
	J.E. Waite		P.F.H. Middleton
			G. Nicholson
			A. Sunderland
M.I.D.—O.Rs.			G.F. Wilks
W.O.I.	K. Berger		G.J.T. Bond
	H. Coussins		J. Flynn
	E.L. Maples		J.W. Bye
	E.F. O'Brien		N.T. Bladon
	A.R.W. Pearce		M.G. Corbett
	H.E. Read		F.R.C. Harrison
	N.J. Vanner		J.C. Hogg
	L. Dale		R.J. Nicholls
	S. Hague		P. Wyatt
	I.S. Scott		G. Chaplin
	J.S. Challoner		H.A. Holmes
	J.H. Clarricoates		P. McCallum
	A.S. Harcourt		L. Pollitt
	W.E.M. Phillips		F. Dickenson
	J. Robinson	C.Q.M.S.	E. Hartshorn
	V.C. Scott	S/Sgt.	E.V. Goldsack
	D.R.O. D'Oyly Watkins	,,	F. Hobson
	E. Wilson		E. Langston
	J. Hay		H. Gardner
	R.A. Hitchman		G.H. Hitchman
	G.E. Jenkins		R.C. Lees
	F. Bailey		I. Lerman
	R.J. Blakenell		F. Mills
	S.G. Chidley		A.A. Holderness
	R.A. Clark		A.B. Woolley
	T.L. Cook		C.S. Braithwaite
	J.G. Fairman		L.F. Brown
	V.W. Groom		A. Caygill
	M. Heap		D.H.S. Griffiths
	W.J. Hornibrook		E.T. Miller
	A. Major		N.S. Robinson
	R.J. Morgan	,,	N.R.S. Tichener
	W.G.R. Pearce	Sgt.	T. Addis
	G.T.W. Shingleton	,,	L.F. Churchward
	R.H.W. Taylor	,,	D. Flower
	F. Thomas		L. Miller
	W.A. Mansell		J.L. Pitt
	H.G. Wheway		R.F Tweed
	A. Wilkinson		F.J. Walker
	C.V. Purbrick		W.K. Williams
	D.F. Scott		T.H. Gribble
	G.A. Stoner		J. Beavers
,, W.O.II.	L.C. Amey		G.H. Botley
	L. Blackett		J.W. Clarke
	C.N. Brook		J. Fletcher
	E.J. Carter		T.A. Gibson

Sgt.	T.H. Gillett	Pte.	J.T.R. Marshall
	E. Jukes		A.E. Bryant
	F.J. Martin		D. Cowie
	F.C. Messenger		K.J. Darrington
	W.G. Watts		J. Donald
	J. Weir		L.G. Hanson
	J.C. Woolrich		E.V. Hogsflesh
	C.H. Greenway		B.H. Rodgers
	J.L. Harvey		A. Sorrie
	A. Blurton		
	F.J. Cahill		
	J.H. Denton		
	E. English		
	D. Ginger		
	K. Griffin		
	F.H. King		
	W.R. Morgan		
	L. Rothwell		
	F.E. Yeomans		
L/Sgt.	D.D. Birkett		
	F.J.R. Abrams		
"	P. Graetz		
Cpl.	J. Gilbert		
	L.A. Ward		
	E. Burnett		
	A. Emmett		
	L. Gallimore		
	A.J. Grigg		
	P.F. Harris		
	J. Kay		
	C.A. Nelson		
	A.C. Ridley		
	G.W. Trehane		
	I.E.G. Ballam		
	H.F. Cadwallader		
	R. Irwin		
	F.N. Miller		
	A. Savidge		
	E. Walker		
	S.T. Eynon		
L/Cpl.	W. Moore		
	E.W. Carter		
	J.F. Marshall		
	P. Phillips		
	J. Ranger		
	H. Gunter		
	J.W. Land		
"	C.O. Newrick		
Pte.	M.M. Clark		
	B.E. Dennis		
	R.H.R. Harman		
	L. Holroyd		
	W. Thom		
	E.J.G. Clack		
	C. Clark		
	J. Davies		
	G. James		
	R. Mandeville		

Canadian Army

M.I.D.—Officers

Lt.Col.	R.T. Bennett
"	M. Mirsky
Maj.	W.E. Bawden
"	H. Denis-Nathan
Capt.	W.A. Armstrong
	R.E. Boykowich
	D.J. Casey
	H.F. Dixon
	G.C. Douglas
	W.J. Finney
	A.S. Findlater, B.E.M.
	G.F. Grainger
	C.R. Harris
	I.C. Heggie
	L.C. Luke
	R.C. Howard
"	S.N. McLean
Lieut.	F.W. Magee

M.I.D.—O.Rs.

W.O.I	G.A. Candler
	E.H. Casselman
	F.B. Raby
	F.G. Webb
W.O.II.	R.H. Calder
	D.L. Harris
	E. Richards
	B.K. Ashley
"	H.J. Doyle
S/Sgt.	M.A. Curruthers
	R.H. Hagan
	W.F. Kidd
"	G.T. Fairbrother
Sgt.	N.J. Burak
	S.O. Gifford
	W.H. Gray
	I. Jonatanson
	R. McEvoy
	A. McNeely
	G.L. Martin
	G.S. Sinclair
	J.V. Sloan

Cpl.	J.R. Dean	L/Cpl.	W.L.G. Francis
	J.A. Graham	,,	D.C. Skerritt
	W.F.J. Cornwell	Pte.	C.D. Adams
	H.L. Griffiths		R.J. Christian
	G.F. Miller		R.W. Crossman
,,	N.D. Stewart		C. Ewing
L/Cpl.	L.A. Burke		F.W. Harris
	O.H. Defresne		

ORDER OF BATTLE OF RAOC UNITS IN 21 ARMY GROUP

Ordnance Beach Detachments

7 O.B.D.
9
10
11
12
14
15
36

Ordnance Field Parks

1 Corps and Army Troops Sub Park.
1 Canadian Corps and Army Troops Sub Park.
2 ,, ,, ,, ,,
3 ,, ,, ,, ,,
8 Corps and Army Troops Sub Park.
12
30

103 Infantry Ordnance Sub Park.
115
143
149
150
151
152
153 ,, ,, ,, ,,
201 Canadian Infantry Ordnance Sub Park.
202
203

107 Armoured Ordnance Sub Park.
111
159
204
205

Guards Ordnance Sub Park

1 Corps Ordnance Field Park.
8
12
30

1 Canadian Corps Ordnance Field Park.
2   ,,

1 Airborne Ordnance Field Park.
6

1 Canadian Infantry Division Ordnance Field Park.
2
3

4 Canadian Armoured Division Ordnance Field Park.
5

3 Division Ordnance Field Park.
5
7
11
15
43
49
50
51
52
53
59

  Guards Division Ordnance Field Park.

1 Canadian Armoured Brigade Ordnance Field Park.
2   ,,

1 Armoured Brigade Ordnance Field Park.
4
8
27
30
31
33
34

6 Guards Brigade Ordnance Field Park.

35 Tank Brigade Ordnance Field Park.

1 Armoured Engineer Brigade Ordnance Field Park.

Advanced Ordnance Depots

14 A.O.D.
15
16
17

Ammunition Depots and Companies

HQ 1 Base Ammunition Depot.
    2   ,,
    3
   12
   15
   17

2 Ordnance Ammunition Company.
3
9
10
14
15
36
37
38
43
44
45
46
50

11 Independent Ordnance Ammunition Company.
32
39
49
51
52
53
54

3 Field Ammunition Repair Factory.

21 Mobile Ammunition Repair Unit.
22   ,,
23
24
25
41
48

1 Canadian Mobile Ammunition Repair Unit.
2

Vehicle Companies

C.O.O. Vehicle Companies.

HQ 14 Vehicle Company.
    141
    142
    143
    144   ,,   ,,
    145 Transit Vehicle Park.
    146 Return   ,,
    147 Vehicle Park.

HQ 15 Vehicle Company.
    151 Vehicle Park.
    152
    153
    154   ,,   ,,
    155 Transit Vehicle Park.
    156 Return   ,,
    157 Vehicle Park.

HQ 16 Vehicle Company.
    161 Vehicle Park.
    162
    163
    164   ,,   ,,
    165 Transit Vehicle Park.
    166 Return Vehicle Park.
    167 Vehicle Park.

HQ 17 Vehicle Company.
    171 Vehicle Park.
    172
    173
    174   ,,   ,,
    175 Transit Vehicle Park.
    176 Return Vehicle Park.
    177 Vehicle Park.

1 Canadian Corps Reserve Vehicle Park.

1 Canadian Special Vehicle Company.

Laundry and Bath Units

1 Canadian Mobile Laundry and Bath Unit.
2
3
4
5
6
7
8
9   ,,   ,,   ,,   ,,

8 Mobile Laundry and Bath Unit.
17
35
54
101
102
104
105
106
107
108
109
301
302
303
304
305
306
307
308
309
310
311

  2 Base Hospital Laundry.
  3   ,,
  4

34 Base Laundry.
35

103 Independent Bath Unit.
110

103 Independent Laundry Unit.
110

13 Mobile Bath Unit.
71
74

Industrial Gas Units

31 A.I.G.U.
32
33
34
51

1 B.I.G.U.
3

Port Ordnance Detachments

31 Port Ordnance Detachment.
32
33
34
35
36
37
38
39
40
41
42
43
44
45
46
47
48
49
50
51
52
53
150

31 Port Ammunition Detachment.
32
33
34
35
36
37
38

39 Port Ammunition Detachment.
40
41
42
43
44
45
46
47
48
49
50
51
52
53

Forward Maintenance Ammunition Sections

1 Canadian Forward Maintenance Ammunition Section.
2
3
4
5

9 Forward Maintenance Ammunition Section.
30
31
50
51
52
53
54
55
56
57
58
59
60
61
63
64
65
66
70
71
72
73

Forward Maintenance Stores Sections

1 Canadian Forward Maintenance Stores Section.
2
3
4

7 Forward Maintenance Stores Section.
40
41

50 Forward Maintenance Stores Section.
51
52
53
54
55
56
57
58
59
60
61
62
63
64
67
68
69
70
71
72

Officers' Shops

50 Officers' Mobile Shop.
51
52
53

1 Canadian Mobile Officers' Shop.
2
3

1 Officers' Shop Company.
31

Miscellaneous

2 Armoured Stores Company
100 Ordnance Company (A.L.M.U.)
1 Canadian Ordnance Maintenance Company
1 Ordnance Maintenance Company
4 ,, ,,
1 Ordnance Stores Depot (CA).

INDEX

A.

	Page
Advanced Base, D.O.S. earmarks units for	32
Advanced Ordnance Depot, arrival of No. 14	28
Advanced Ordnance Depot, first recce party drowned	26, 34
Advanced Ordnance Depot, grading of issues in beachhead	29
Advanced Ordnance Depot, No. 15, arrival of	29
Advanced Ordnance Depot, original plans for	14
Advanced Ordnance Depot, record of each A.O.D.	34
A.Ds.O.S., part played in planning	12
Airborne Divisions, Ordnance services for	66
Ammunition, daily tonnage received over beaches.	26
Ammunition, tonnage handled from D-day to the end of February	33
Ammunition Depots, No. 17 Base opened	26
Ammunition Depots, original plans for	15
Ammunition Depots, record of Ammunition Depots and Roadheads	43
Ammunition Repair Units, work done by	63
Antwerp, Ordnance receipts arrive through	49
Arctic, conditions, Ordnance stores to meet	50
Ardennes, counter-attack, effect on Ordnance	49
Armoured Stores Company, how served Armoured Replacement Group	61
Arnhem, Ordnance airborne personnel drop at	67
Army Group, Appreciation fulfilment of	32
Army Group, Ordnance Directorate's first Appreciation	29

B.

Belsen, early arrival of Bath and Laundry units	60
Beach Maintenance Packs, preparation of	14
Beach Sub Areas, absorbed into B.M.A.	26
Beach Sub Areas, Ordnance plan for	14
Beach Sub Areas, Ordnance units serving	19
B.O.W.O.'s, part played in planning	12

C.

Canadian Ordnance Corps, brilliant record of	73
Cansdale, Major-General C., appointed D.O.S.	56
Cape, Colonel J.R.M., as D.D.O.S.	10

Page

C.

Capitulation, Ordnance problems arising out of	54
Central Ordnance Depots, work of	9, 10, 33
Churchill, Mr. Winston, announces landing on Continent	9
Churchill, Mr. Winston, on equipment for Invasion	9
Clarke's, Brigadier T.H., original Appreciation	16
Clothing and Necessaries, importance in battle	28
Convoy Units, Advanced Ordnance formed	53
Convoy Units, formed by 15 F.T.S.	29
Convoy Units, work done by	64
Corps Field Parks, first into theatre	16
Corps Field Parks, position on D+18	30
Corps Field Parks, representative range of stores and issues	54
Cutforth, Brigadier L.E., as D.D.O.S.	10, 56

D.

D-day, adventures of Ordnance units	20
D-day, maintenance of assault force during	16
D-day, Ordnance airborne service for	66
D.A.D.O.S. Dumps, service given by	63
Denniston, Brigadier J.G., appointed D.O.S.	10
Depot Control Companies, activities of	65
Divisional Ordnance Field Parks, elastic organisation	54
Divisional Ordnance Field Parks, first into theatre	16
Divisional Ordnance Field Parks, position on D+18	30
D.Ds.O.S., part played in planning	12

F.

Forward Maintenance, record of Stores and Ammunition Sections	61
Forward Trailer Sections, allocated to First and Second Armies	32
Forward Trailer Sections, how used	62

G.

Gas Units, Army and Base, record of	60
Grigg, Sir James, on Invasion preparations by Ordnance	10

	Page

H.

Hospital service, Ordnance plans for maintenance of	58

I.

Invasion, Ordnance planning for	11

J.

"Jantzen Exercise"	15

K.

King, Brigadier H., as D.O.S.	10

L.

Landing Reserves, scaling and packing of	14
Laundries, record of M.L.B.U.'s	57
Laundries, work of Base Laundries and Base Hospital Laundries	58
Local Procurement, Ordnance stores provided by	65
L of C., growth effects A.O.D.	36
L of C. problems raised by sudden expansion	32

M.

Maintenance Companies, at Army Roadheads	62
Montgomery, General, on equipment for Invasion	9

O.

Ordnance Ammunition Companies, first to arrive	15
Ordnance Beach Detachments, disbanded personnel given new tasks	26
Ordnance Beach Detachments, First into theatre	15
Ordnance Maintenance Companies, arrival in theatre	16
"Overlord, Operation", Ordnance planning for	11

P.

Pas-de-Calais Ports, Ordnance receipts through	33
Planning, Joint British and American staff formed	9
"Plunder", Ordnance Airborne service for operation	67
"Plunder", Ordnance units participating in operation	51

	Page
P.	
"Plunder", special equipments and stores for operation .	51
Port Ammunition Detachments, first into theatre .	16
Port Ordnance Detachments first into theatre	16
R.	
"Rankin" Operation, Ordnance plans for	12
Regimental training in preparation for Invasion	10
Returned Stores, how handled in bridgehead	28
Reichswald Forest, see "Veritable" Operation	50
Rhine Crossing, see "Plunder" Operation	51
Road Maintenance Teams, formed by Ordnance	40
S.	
Second Army, Ordnance plan to support up to D+17	16
Shops, Officers', record of	64
"Snowball" Exercise .	15
Stores, Ordnance, how delivered to airborne Divisions	67
Stores, Ordnance, tonnage handled from D-day to the end of February	33
Stores, Ordnance, range of .	9
Swiney, Brigadier C.A.N., as D.O.S.	10
T.	
Training Establishment, Leicester, 21 Army Group Conference	12
V.	
Vehicles, handled from D-day to the end of February	33
Vehicles, range of, makes and types	40
"Veritable", Ordnance preparations for Operation	50
"Veritable", Ordnance units participating in Operation	50
W.	
Williams, Major-General L.H., revises Ordnance organisation	10

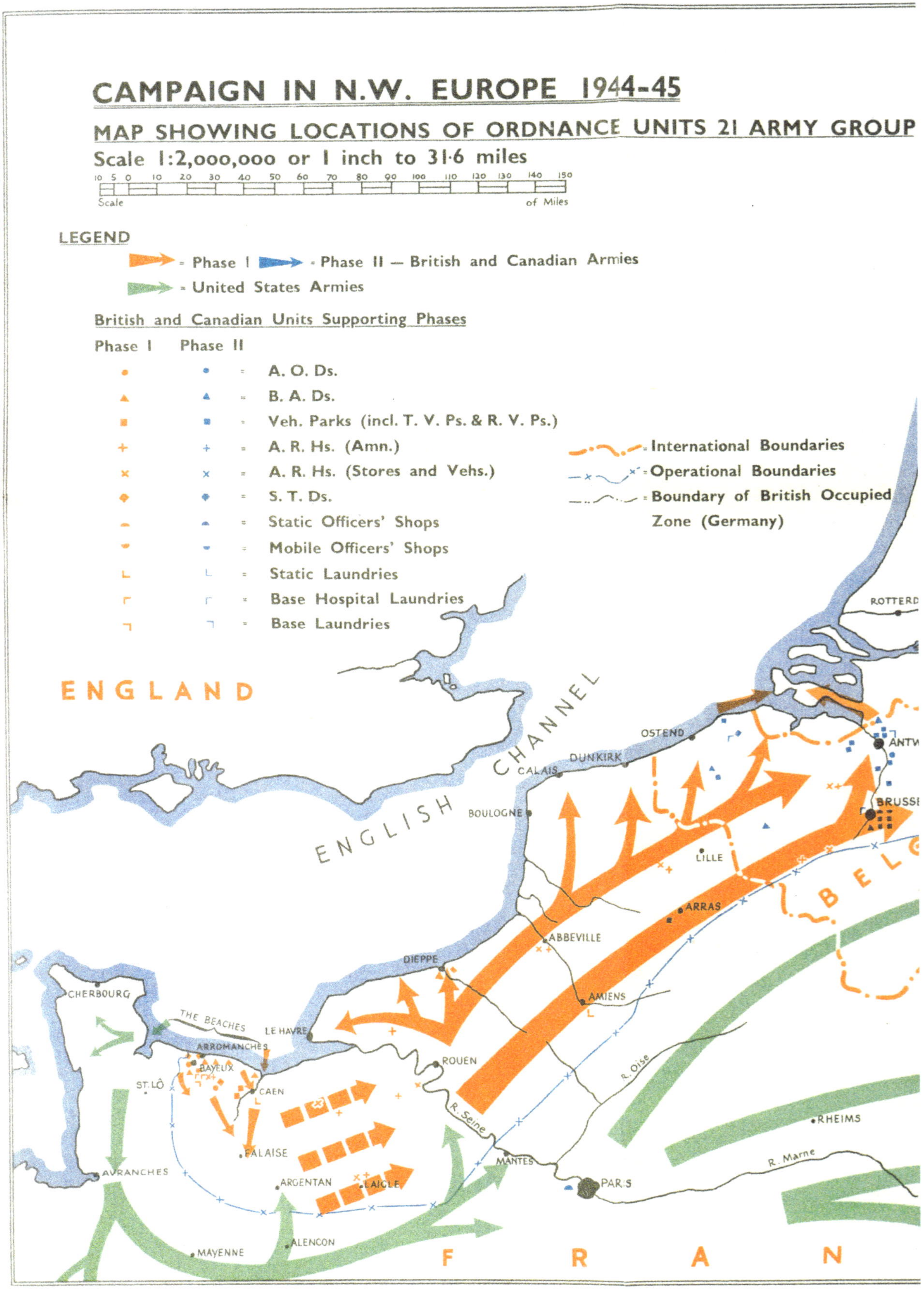
CAMPAIGN IN N.W. EUROPE 1944-45
MAP SHOWING LOCATIONS OF ORDNANCE UNITS 21 ARMY GROUP
Scale 1:2,000,000 or 1 inch to 31·6 miles
10 5 0 10 20 30 40 50 60 70 80 90 100 110 120 130 140 150
Scale of Miles
LEGEND
= Phase I
= Phase II — British and Canadian Armies
= United States Armies
British and Canadian Units Supporting Phases
Phase I
Phase II
= A. O. Ds.
= B. A. Ds.
= Veh. Parks (incl. T. V. Ps. & R. V. Ps.)
= A. R. Hs. (Amn.)
= A. R. Hs. (Stores and Vehs.)
= S. T. Ds.
= Static Officers' Shops
= Mobile Officers' Shops
= Static Laundries
= Base Hospital Laundries
= Base Laundries
= International Boundaries
= Operational Boundaries
= Boundary of British Occupied Zone (Germany)
ENGLAND
ENGLISH CHANNEL
ROTTERD
OSTEND
DUNKIRK
CALAIS
BOULOGNE
ANTW
BRUSSE
LILLE
ARRAS
ABBEVILLE
DIEPPE
AMIENS
CHERBOURG
THE BEACHES
LE HAVRE
ARROMANCHES
BAYEUX
ST. LÔ
CAEN
ROUEN
R. Seine
R. Oise
RHEIMS
FALAISE
MANTES
PARIS
R. Marne
AVRANCHES
ARGENTAN
L'AIGLE
MAYENNE
ALENCON
BELG
FRAN

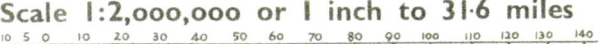

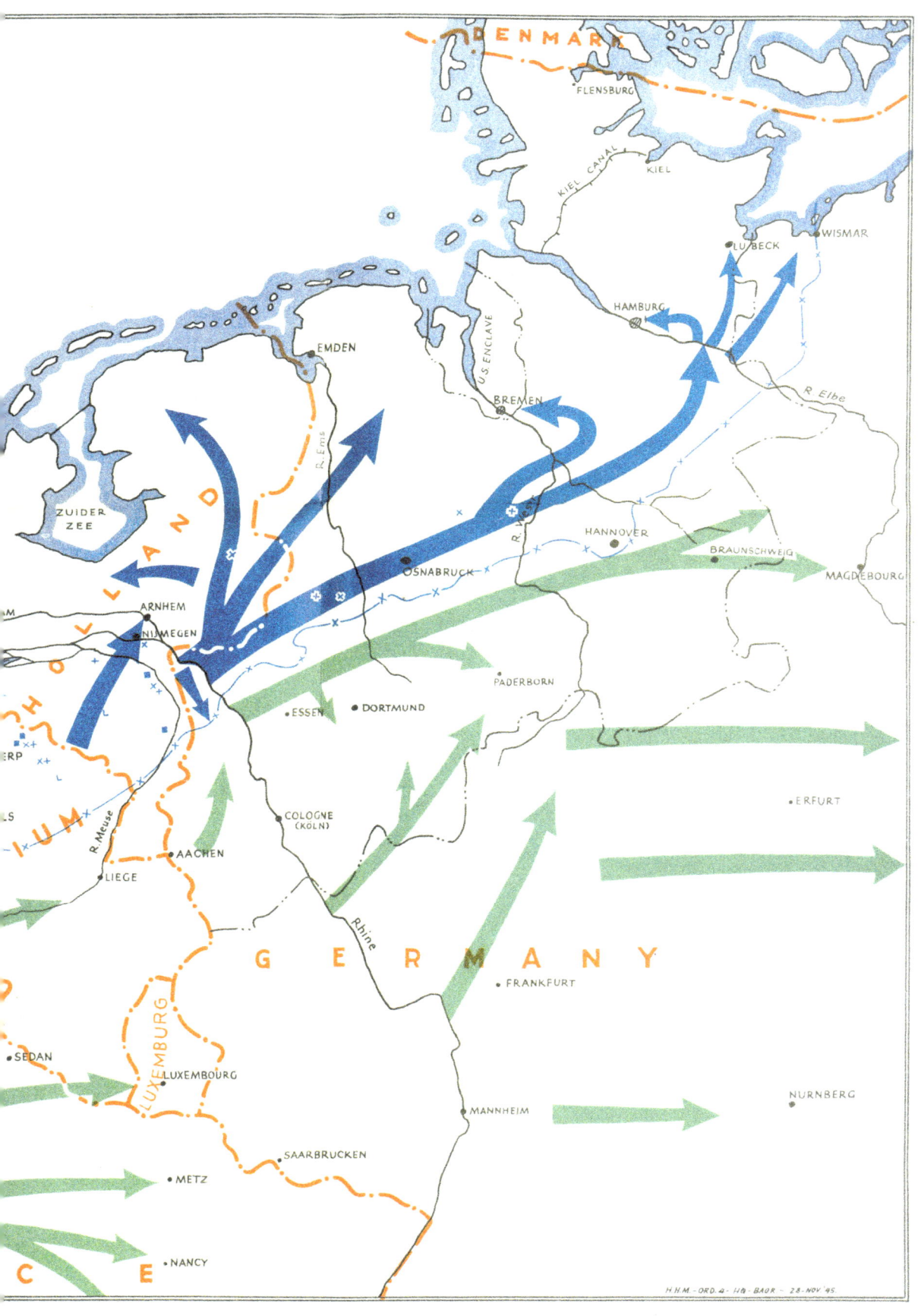

www.ingramcontent.com/pod-product-compliance
Lightning Source LLC
Chambersburg PA
CBHW060931180426
43192CB00045B/2891